Finding the
SACRED SELF

A SHAMANIC WORKBOOK

DR. SUSAN GREGG

1995
LLEWELLYN PUBLICATIONS
ST. PAUL, MINNESOTA 55164-0383, U.S.A.

FIRST EDITION
Second Printing, 1995

Cover painting and design: Anne Marie Garrison
Interior illustrations: Wendy Frogge't
Editing, design, and layout: Pamela Henkel

Library of Congress Cataloging-in-Publication Data

Gregg, Susan, 1949—
    Finding the sacred self : a shamanic workbook /
    by Susan Gregg.
    p.   cm.
    ISBN 1-56718-334-4
    1. Shamanism. 2. Spiritual exercises. I. Title.
    BF1611.G76   1995
    291.1'4—dc20   94-47131
                                     CIP

Llewellyn Publications
A Division of Llewellyn Worldwide, Ltd.
P.O. Box 64383, St. Paul, MN 55164-0383

DEDICATION

This book is dedicated to the love that lives within us all.

TABLE OF
▲▲▲ CONTENTS ▲▲▲

ACKNOWLEDGMENTS

I would like to acknowledge all the people who have touched my life in so many different ways. The lessons I have learned from them have not always been easy but they have always led to a greater sense of freedom and joy.

I would like to thank Richard, whose prodding has at times driven me crazy but has pushed me to grow. I love you, my friend. June, thank you for making my new computer possible when the old one blew up, right in the middle of this book. To all my friends and clients who have encouraged me, especially the people who have come to explore and stayed to share.

I would also like to thank all my teachers and my parents, without them I wouldn't be here. Dad, thanks for believing in me even when I couldn't.

I would also like to thank Hawaii for its warm waters, gentle trade winds, and its numerous rainbows. And of course, thank you for reading this book.

Life sure is grand.

▲▲▲ INTRODUCTION ▲▲▲

I spent much of my early life seeking. There always seemed to be something missing in my life; it seemed flat, empty, somehow unrewarding. No matter what I achieved externally, how successful I was, what I did or who I was with, there was always a deep sense of yearning—of wanting something more.

I had begun meditating in the early '70s but I avidly avoided anything spiritual or religious. Quite a few of my friends had become "born again" and couldn't talk about anything else. Once they were "religiously enlightened," everything I did was wrong or sinful. Between that and my early experiences with hell fire and brimstone, I avoided anything with religious overtones. The longer I meditated the deeper my sense of yearning became, but I refused to explore the difference between spirituality and religion. I tried to find higher highs. I didn't know what I wanted, I just knew I wanted more.

I never knew what that "more" was until long after I met and began studying with Miguel and Sarita. I knew I wanted inner peace but I wasn't sure what inner peace was or how to find it. I wasn't actually sure what I was looking for; I still believed my happiness came from outside myself. Even after I started studying with Miguel and Sarita I wasn't sure why I was there or what I wanted. I just wanted the inner pain to stop; I wanted to stop feeling driven. It wasn't until years later that I understood what I had been searching for.

As much as I hated to admit it, spirituality was the very thing that was missing from my life. That sense of emptiness came from my isolation from anything sacred. I had lost my connection to the Creator, earth, and everything spiritual.

I have come to realize that life is a process of reclaiming that connection; it unfolds daily in my life. I now know that I had always been searching for *myself*—for a sense of connection and oneness with the whole. In the past I believed that I would find my happiness in people, places, or things. I always defined my happiness as something that existed externally. I spent years looking for someone or something that could fix me. I certainly didn't believe I could fix myself by changing my perspective. I knew that I would be happy as soon as I got to my destination, once I made "X" dollars, found the right lover, or had the perfect ____. *Then* I would be happy. I never thought that happiness was actually part of the process.

Today I define happiness as a sense of peace, a feeling of being one, being safe, and feeling loved completely and unconditionally. It is something I can experience each moment of my life if I choose to alter my perception of the world. Happiness is a way of life, an inner sense of peace and joy—a knowing beyond mere belief that everything is okay and that I am safe, loved, and accepted unconditionally.

I spent years searching for that feeling. Ironically, what I been had searching for so desperately had always been within my grasp. Just like the characters in *The Wizard of Oz,* I already had the very things I had been searching for. Like Dorothy I always had the ability to "go home"; I just didn't know it.

I had believed that happiness was created by circumstances beyond my control. In a sense, I felt that my happiness was a victim of circumstance. Consequently, I kept searching outside myself, and I came up short.

Today I know that my happiness originates within myself. Now I know that I can choose to be happy whenever I want to be because I am the only one who is in "control" of it. I am responsible for my own happiness. It has nothing to do with anyone or anything else. External events can only affect me if I allow them.

I define the sacred self as the part of you that knows life is an illusion, but understands fully how sacred and precious every experience is. It lives in love. The sacred self has reverence for everyone and everything. It is the essence of who and what you are, and life is most fulfilling when you are connected with your true divinity.

To be truly happy and free you must find your own path, honor your process, and then have the courage and conviction to follow it. The way I teach is very different from the way Miguel taught me and I am sure that the way Miguel taught is different from the way his teachers taught him. Each one of you has your own process; if you learn to honor it—if you find your sacred space and that place within yourself that is always at peace—then and only then are you truly free.

This book is a series of exercises designed to assist you in changing your perspective and the way you interact with your world. They are designed to assist you in finding your own sense of happiness and personal freedom. As you work with these exercises you will begin to realize that happiness is a state of mind that you can create whenever you want. But you can only do that once you know that you are free to choose and know how to choose. This workbook is designed to show you how to create that sense of freedom in your life. It is designed to assist you in finding your own process or path, and learning how to honor it.

This book will assist you in honoring and connecting with your sacred nature. I will lead you through many of the processes I went through during my studies with Miguel. However, I will focus more on the sacred aspects I learned later from his mother and other women.

The exercises are designed to help you experience and connect with that sacred place within you. My personal freedom began when I stopped looking for answers outside of myself and I began looking within. Learning to trust yourself is the greatest gift you can give yourself, and it was one of the most frightening things I ever did. At one point I stopped looking toward Miguel and others in my life for answers. It felt like I had gone beyond my teachers. I felt alone and terrified that I wouldn't be able to do it. Eventually, I realized that the only one who could set me free was myself. As I reclaimed my personal power and connected with that place of knowing, I knew that the Creator lived within me and I was one with that energy.

That place of knowing resides within our feminine nature. Society places a great deal of emphasis on doing, actively creating, and achieving. It honors the male side of our humanness and teaches us to neglect our feminine, intuitive, or spiritual side. This book is designed to assist all human beings in reclaiming their gentle, loving, intuitive sacred self.

I hope you will find that place within yourself and begin finding your own answers. If you get nothing else from this book, please learn to honor your process and honor the divinity that you already are.

Life is like a flower bud that is gently unfolding. Given time and the proper conditions, that bud becomes a beautiful flower. But if we get impatient and pull apart the petals we end up with a mess. Allow your process, your life, to unfold for you gently and lovingly.

When I am living from my sacred self, life is a magnificent journey. When I am living from my head, I once again have an endless list of unfulfilled desires. Join me in learning how to live from that sacred self. In my earlier book *The Dance of Power,* I describe my apprenticeship with Miguel and Sarita. In this book I will share many of the exercises that assisted me in connecting with that sacred self. You can use these exercises alone or with a group. I suggest getting a journal so you can record your progress and your process.

The exercises in this book reflect my process and the way I teach my students. After you have worked with them for a-while adapt them as you see fit but at first I suggest you follow the directions carefully. Quite often your mind will try to distract you with short cuts or easier ways to do things. Often these short cuts are your mind's ways of protecting yourself from the truth.

Find a trusted partner to share this process with—one who will allow you to have your feelings and not judge your process. It is much easier to see the truth when someone else is available to act as a mirror for you. But it is better to do the exercises alone than never to do them at all.

What stands between you and your sacred self is a set of beliefs, a great number of feelings, and your mind's needless protection of your ego. Begin to explore that sacred place and find your way home.

I once had a dream about two worlds, one of which I called Utopia. It was a world in which everyone lived from their sacred centers. This world was wonderful, completely peaceful, and magical. The only difference between the two worlds was in their perspectives and beliefs—one world lived from its head and the other lived from its sacred center. Otherwise the people were the same.

What would your life be like if you knew you were totally safe at all times and felt loved unconditionally by everyone, including yourself? How would you feel if you knew everyone was truly honored to be in your presence and truly liked you? What would your life be like today if you had known that since birth?

Now imagine for a moment what your life would be like if each moment were a sacred act. What would life be like if no matter where you were or what you were doing, you were aware of the sacredness and you felt that sense of safety and love? What if each moment of your life was lived with passion and you loved everything about your life? How would you feel right now if that were true?

When we know that our lives are sacred, everything changes, yet nothing changes. Finding and living from our sacred selves is a profound act that can change the world. It can be a gentle and loving process. Join me in finding your sacred self.

In love and light.

CHAPTER ONE

THE BEGINNING

Two apprentices, a man and a woman, were walking down a path late one night. The moon was moving toward full, but not yet bright enough to dim the stars. The wind rapidly pushed the clouds as they danced over the face of the moon. The shadows they created moved ominously over the high desert terrain.

The night was far from empty; many spirits were out. The apprentices hurried along. The quiet was almost deafening, only broken by the sound of their footsteps in the loose gravel and the occasional cricket. Off in the distance a coyote howled.

They spoke in whispers about the lessons they had learned. Their teacher had unexpectedly told them to return home tonight. They had never been asked to leave after dark before. Their teacher had laughed at their fear. They tried to be warriors as they walked along the path but fear continued to rise to the surface. They knew someone was lurking in the darkness waiting for them.

As they approached the path leading toward the cliff they thought they saw someone step out of the shadows. At first they laughed at their foolishness but then they began to hear a quiet chanting. Before them stood an ancient one. Only terror held them in place.

The old one said, "Who do we have here? Who comes before me? Come closer and let me see you."

Slowly they both began to inch backward. They had heard stories of the old ones and how they steal the unsuspecting apprentice's souls. Their hearts began pounding and fear began to rise within them; the night was filled with the sound of their breathing.

The old one asked, "What do you fear? Certainly not one as old as me, alone in the desert. How could I possibly harm you? Are you victims or warriors?"

The man timidly began to speak, "I have heard stories of the old ones and how they steal people's souls. I have no wish to fight you."

The old one laughed and said, "Who asked you to fight me? Do you really believe those stories meant to scare children into listening to their elders? Come closer so I can see you."

Again they edged back and the woman asked, "Why are you here? Who are you and what do you want?"

The ancient one smiled and said, "The path to freedom always leads through your fears. You can never be free until you have faced your fears and conquered them. Your healing and your sacred self lies in the direction your head tells you not to go. Whenever your head says, 'I will not do this,' you must do it or you will never be truly free. Listen not to your head; listen always to your heart."

The man said, "Those are fine words, old one, but they sound like words of a trickster to me. Why should I trust you?"

"Because your mind tells you not to," replied the ancient one. "Listen to your heart; what does it tell you? Come closer so I can see you."

For a moment they all stood motionless on the edge of the cliff. Before the man had a chance to stop her, the woman smiled and stepped forward. The man yelled "No," but the woman and the ancient one just smiled.

Then the old one reached out and in a rapid, fluid movement, pushed her off the cliff. And she flew.

▼▼▼

Any time we attempt to change our core beliefs, it feels like we are jumping off into nothingness. I have one client who is fond of saying, "You are trying to get me to step off that cliff again." I remember my own fear whenever Miguel would try to get me to look at the world in a new way. I would resist with all my might but my spiritual self, my feminine side, would push me to take the leap in spite of my fear. Those quantum leaps always changed me and my perspective profoundly.

My view of the world these days is entirely different than it used to be. I was born and raised in New York City and was accustomed to being very active. I didn't know much about just *being*. When I was in high school my family moved to a rural town in northern Vermont. I felt like a fish out of water, but eventually I fell in love with the beauty and serenity of the country. The contrast between how I felt inside and the beauty outside made me realize that there was something missing in my life. I had lost myself somewhere along the way. By then I believed that life was a struggle, and that what you see is what you get.

In my thirties I moved to southern California where I met the people who were to become my teachers, Miguel and Sister Sarita. They didn't speak English and I didn't speak Spanish, yet their presence in my life managed to totally change the direction of my reality. In the '70s I had read Carlos Castaneda's books. I was fascinated but found them very unsettling, and I certainly had no desire to meet such a teacher. In Miguel I met that teacher, and in the process I learned to look at the world in an entirely different manner. My life changed completely.

Miguel came from a long line of Naguals, medicine men or sorcerers who understand how the universe operates. Their knowledge can be traced back to the Toltecs. Miguel's grandfather was a powerful Nagual and had told Sarita, Miguel's mother, that her son would follow in the tradition. She found that hard to believe because Miguel had already become a successful surgeon. While he was doing his community service in the interior of Mexico, Miguel began to study with a Nagual. A few years later he left his lucrative medical practice and joined Sarita in the United States and became a spiritual healer instead.

I studied with Miguel and Sarita for several years before I had a clear idea what I was studying or why. Miguel would talk about breaking this reality and personal freedom and the only thing I knew for sure was that life as I knew it was no longer working—it was falling apart. Slowly I began to see the world differently. He never talked to me about the sacred self or where we were going, so I had no idea what was happening or what I needed to do. We came from such different cultures and backgrounds that he was often puzzled by my confusion. He believed in a hostile universe; I was beginning to "know" it was loving and safe.

In retrospect, I realize that my philosophy about life was changing as well as my perspective. I was redefining my definitions of how life worked and changing the rules. I began to see how my life actually operated, began to see how my old philosophy had only caused me pain. I realized that any limitations in my life were due to my old beliefs. I needed to change them if I wanted to get different results.

Making these changes was difficult for me because I wasn't sure what was happening. I felt confused most of the time. My confusion was probably very useful because it kept my mind out of the way. I have come to realize that my mind would rather be right than happy. At some level it is more comfortable for people to remain the same rather than to change, even if they are not happy.

The only way to easily overcome fear is to connect with your spirituality. Because of my intense aversion to anything religious or spiritual, I struggled much more than was necessary with many of these concepts. At any cost, I tried to stay in my head and avoid my feelings and intuitive nature. That decision caused me a great deal of pain. In a sense I fought the process all the way. My narrow definition of religion didn't allow for a distinction between religion and spirituality.

I now have a very different philosophy about life. I know that something is in charge of the universes, and it isn't I. As I remain in harmony with that force, miracles happen in my life. Today I know that the universe is a friendly and supportive place; it is no longer out to get me.

Miguel's basic philosophy is that we are not physical bodies; we are energy within the bodies. Everything in this universe is composed of energy, and that energy has consciousness. It is that consciousness that is often referred to as God or the Great Spirit. I prefer to think of that energy as the Creator.

Miguel stressed that the goal was to achieve personal freedom, defined as the ability to flourish anywhere. He talked a lot about energy, about being able to feel it and manipulate it. He taught from a male perspective of doing and action. Sarita would smile in mild annoyance and talk about spirituality, being receptive, and about the Creator's will for us to be happy and of service to others—the female perspective.

At one time I thought personal freedom meant having lots of money. Now it means knowing myself, having inner peace, and among other things, feeling a sense of harmony with my world. I'm not sure why, but in the process of changing my perspective, money also became more plentiful. I have learned to do things for the sake of doing them. My mind tells me to do things only if I will get something in return. Now I find that taking an action in order to get something always seems to backfire.

When I was studying with Miguel most of the things we did made no sense to me. I was constantly asking Miguel why. He would smile, but would seldom answer my questions directly. I didn't understand why I should become sensitive to the energies around me or why I should meditate in front of a mirror, but I did the exercises anyway. My mind couldn't understand the concept of other realities or accept my experiences of them. I now realize that those alternative universes do exist and they are just as real as ours.

My beliefs about my physical body and the reality of physicality itself were often challenged during my studies. At one point Miguel cured a chronic back problem. Another time I went to class with the beginning of the flu; everyone I knew who had had it was sick for at least a week. I was feeling sick and couldn't stop coughing. I coughed throughout class and finally asked Miguel if I should leave. He shook his head and had me sit in the center of the circle. The other students put their hands on me and we all began to meditate. I immediately stopped coughing and never caught the flu.

I saw many miraculous healings throughout my studies. Miguel or Sarita often performed psychic surgery and then told the people to come back later to have their stitches out. I could handle psychic surgery, but not invisible stitches.

My rational, linear mind had a very difficult time with most of these concepts. They were so far beyond my "normal" experiences of the way life operated that my mind was unable to understand them, much less explain them. As you practice some of the exercises in this book you may find yourself having the same reaction. Listen to your heart, not your head. This path, as with most spiritual paths, often requires a leap of faith. Our answers always lie in our hearts, or our sacred selves—an area our minds seldom enter.

As you do the exercises in this book try to have an open mind or an attitude of no mind. The Tao describes no mind as a state free of ego, an attitude of openness and acceptance. I think of it as being teachable. Our mind's main function is to keep us safe. It usually defines safe as familiar and explainable. My mind likes to think it has all the answers—it hates to say it doesn't know. Our freedom lies in our ability to say we don't know or to realize that we are not really sure how this world operates. When we remain that open we can receive new information and learn the truth instead of defending our old beliefs and explanations. We can begin to use our personal power to create our reality rather than remain a victim to it.

A Nagual is a person of power, someone who has the ability to create what he or she wants at any given moment. As long as the individual remains in harmony with the universe, his or her power continues to grow. A true person of power lives in the sacred self. The power comes from that center and the connection to his or her source. If the person moves toward the "dark side of the force," his or her power begins to diminish.

Eventually, I found that the only power that is real in this world is spiritual. Any other form of power is just an illusion. When I first began studying about power, I was uncomfortable with the concept. I defined power as the ability to exert control over someone or something. I thought power and control were synonymous, and that people were powerful if they could control others. Power was manipulation.

Nothing could be further from the truth. Manipulation is a misuse of power. When spiritual beings misuse power they automatically cut themselves off from the source of their power. Manipulation and control are tools used by a fearful mind that is listening to a negative ego.

True power comes from being in harmony with the universe and with your connection to your spiritual self. The ancient Hawaiians believed in remaining in harmony with the forces of the universe. If they wanted to move a rock they asked the rock's permission. If the rock gave its permission, then they carried only the rock, not the weight of the rock. If we refuse to ask because we fear that the rocks may say no, we create pain and hardship for ourselves.

During the course of these exercises many of your beliefs and definitions will be challenged and you may find it necessary to question and change many of them. Rather than defending your old beliefs, allow yourself to experience your answers. Begin developing your own beliefs based upon the results that you are achieving in your life. Most of the beliefs you now have are based on ideas that have been given to you by your parents and your environment. One of the first steps you can take toward your personal freedom is to begin choosing your beliefs.

Our minds tend to remember the past and superimpose that remembrance on the present. We seldom truly experience what is happening in the moment. Our minds merely recall a similar event and then "see" reality as it was rather than as it is.

If in the past a lover took you to a restaurant, gave you roses, and then dumped you, you would react very negatively to a new lover giving you roses. Your mind would believe receiving roses meant rejection, when the other person thought it meant he or she loved you. As the Talmud says, we see things not as they are, but as we are.

Allow yourself to start by reprogramming your mind. If your old beliefs weren't limiting your experience of life in some way, you wouldn't be reading this book. Allow yourself to experience how limitless life can be when you let go of the past. You are totally responsible for how you experience your life, but you are not in any way at fault. The old saying that you can be as happy as you make up your mind to be is true, but only after you change your perspective and definitions.

Our reality is colored by our filters. Your mind automatically filters everything you experience through your beliefs and expectations. It is like looking at life through a pair of glasses that blur your vision. No two people experience "reality" in quite the same way. Each person's definitions and beliefs are uniquely theirs. To change your life you must change your perspective; you must remove your filters.

As you practice these exercises you will begin to experience the world more on an energy level. This shift will help you go beyond your mind. As you release the story your mind tells you about everything, you can begin to change your experiences. As your perspective changes, the results you are getting in your life will also change.

At one point during my studies, I was practicing experiencing emotions as energy. One day I began to feel something, and I decided not to label it. If I had labeled it, I would have called it anxiety, but by the end of the day I realized that the feeling was, in reality, excitement. I never would have realized it if I hadn't decided to experience my emotions as energy and not listen to my mind's definition of them. When I realized I was feeling excitement instead of anxiety my experience was certainly much more pleasant.

You have learned to see the world in a certain way and you believe it to be the only way to see it, or at least the only right way. Beliefs are very powerful. Look at how many millions of people have died in wars. A war is caused by two countries with opposing beliefs or perspectives. Each side is equally committed to defending their perspective, they both "know" they are right and the other wrong. As you let go of your beliefs you are able to step beyond many of your limitations.

The world is not at all how we perceive it. From the level of our minds we see everything in terms of duality or separation. There is black and white, right and wrong, good and evil, inside and outside, and me and you. In truth there is no "out there," it is merely a reflection of "in here." "Out there" is created by what you think and believe inside. As you have no doubt heard many times, we are all one—there is no separation. There are no limitations except in our minds.

I may believe or understand ideas I have read or been told. When I have truly felt or experienced something for myself, I know it beyond a shadow of a doubt. This book is about that sense of knowing. Once you really know a truth, it is much easier to live it. I am no longer comfortable living from my mind. When I listen to my head I rapidly lose my peace, serenity, and sense of oneness. When I listen to my heart or sacred self, I am at peace no matter what is going on around me. I don't control all the events in my life but I can certainly choose how I react to them. Do I want to live in love or fear? That choice is always mine.

Many of these exercises might not make sense. How will becoming sensitive to energy change your life? How will meditating in front of a mirror allow you more freedom? Don't worry about why and how, simply do the exercises. Do them just for the sake of doing them, and see what happens. Time and again I have found that I short-change myself whenever I do something for a specific reason or to get a specific result. When I do something merely for the sake of doing it, I am open, receptive, and seem to receive the benefits anyway.

You can do these exercises alone or with a group. It would be useful to do them with at least one other person so you can share your experiences. Keep a journal of the whole process, record your thoughts, feelings, beliefs, etc. Our minds would rather ignore this new information; writing it down helps reduce our mind's denial. It will be interesting for you to see how your life changes over time.

Allow this process to be a gentle one. Take your time with these exercises. It literally took me years to complete them so try not to do them all in one day. They are a gateway to a new way of life, a new way of being in this world.

Try to follow the directions carefully the first time. You may wish to record the meditations on tape or have a friend read them to you. After some of the exercises, I will give you examples of what may happen. If possible, do an exercise first and then read about what may happen so you don't contaminate your experience. If your experience is different, let that be all right. Your experience is your experience. The only reason I include possible outcomes is for reassurance, so you won't think that you are crazy. I often felt that way while I was studying with Miguel. Try not to compare your experiences. Your experiences are uniquely yours. Honor them.

Everyone processes information and experiences ethereal energy in a different manner. Some people see clear pictures, some hear things, and others have an inner feeling. However you do it—whether you feel, see, or hear it—is just fine. Begin right now to honor your process. No one else will live life in the same way you will, just as no one will have the same insights and experiences as they go through these exercises.

At the beginning of each chapter you will find a parable, or a teaching story. Stories are a wonderful tool, they can assist you in changing your perspective in a gentle and subtle manner. As you read these stories, let them work their magic on you. If any have an emotional charge for you, read them again in a few days. The ones you react to either positively or negatively are the ones that challenge your beliefs in some way. There is no need to analyze or argue with them; simply read them, and then read them again. If you don't understand an aspect of one of the stories, trust your process and let it unfold in its own time. For me that step is always a major challenge, but it helps me learn to honor my process.

One of the major goals of this book is to assist you in finding your own answers. These exercises are designed to help you find your sacred self, so trust that you are doing just that. There is no right or wrong way to do this process. When I first began meditating in a group, I would judge my experience harshly. After our meditations, everyone would share what they had experienced. I would mentally tear my experience apart as each person shared, telling myself that my meditation wasn't as deep or profound as the next person's. Treat yourself with more respect and gentleness than I was able to while I was a student. Love and honor yourself and your process from the very start.

Allow this to be a sacred act. Years ago when I opened my first retail store a friend of mine told me to enjoy the process. She said that it would be the only time I would be able to open a store for the first time. She was right, but I was unable to enjoy the process. Now I try to make everything a sacred act, one that I am performing with full consciousness, respect, and love. Give yourself that gift to whatever degree you are willing and able.

You might start the process with the following prayer or a similar one you make up for yourself.

> *Universe, Great Spirit, God, Goddess, all there is. Creator, please hear me. Assist me in honoring my path. Allow this to be a sacred act. I seek to find that sacred self. I wish to know myself and my oneness with you. I seek to find that quiet place where only love resides. Help me, your humble creation, to find the power and wisdom that lives within each of us. Give me the wisdom and strength to release my old way of being in this world. Show me how you would have me live. I ask for your love, your assistance, and your guidance. Please help me to find my way. Allow me to always act in love and to be harmless. Help*

me to enjoy the process. May I live always in love. I open myself to you and humbly ask that my sacredness be revealed to me. So as it has been asked for, so it will be received. I give thanks and ask to be of service to you and those who journey with me. May I walk always in the light and may I always be surrounded and protected by your love. In love.

I start each day with a period of quiet contemplation. I pray and ask for assistance in being closer to my spiritual self and closer to God. I ask to be used as a channel of that love and I surrender my day to that sacred self.

Let the process begin for you.

NOTES

▲▲▲ CHAPTER TWO ▲▲▲

MEDITATION

He had been a seeker all of his life. He had searched the world looking for the truth. He had spent years with many teachers—always looking, always searching, yet never finding. He had dedicated his life to finding God, but he was always restless in his search.

As the years went on, he tried to remain hopeful, but with each passing year it became harder. He had often gone to the top of mountains and yelled at God, asking why he hid from him. At times he felt overwhelmed with the compulsion to search; he would not die without finding God. But, finally, it looked as if he had run out of time.

As he laid all alone on his death bed, he began to cry. He was overwhelmed by an immense sadness; he no longer had the energy to fight. The only thing he could do was surrender to his feelings.

Suddenly an ancient one stood before him. The man rubbed his eyes in amazement. In a frail voice he asked, "Why now? Where have you been all of my life?"

The ancient one answered, "I have always been here. You have been too busy searching to listen. You fought so hard I could not out-shout your mind. You howled so loudly you could only hear yourself."

"What do you mean?" said the man. "I have studied the truth all of my life. My only prayer has been for enlightenment. How dare you say I have been too busy to listen? I have spent all my time searching!"

"Exactly," said the old one. "You had a choice, my friend, to seek with your head or know with your heart. You never sat still long enough to listen."

"I have spent years fighting the emotions of my heart," said the man. "What is there to find in anyone's heart but sentimental drivel? If a student works hard and learns to control his emotions perhaps he will be fortunate enough to find enlightenment. If one suffers long enough and learns to master himself, then and only then will he be master of his fate."

The old one smiled sadly and said, "Do you truly believe you can find enlightenment by controlling things? What of love? What of good works?"

"Love is fine for the masses, but the truly enlightened have no need for emotions. Emotions are a sign of weakness. Good works are for people who have a need to prove themselves; I have no need for other people's good will."

"Let me tell you a story," said the ancient one. The man feebly nodded.

"Once at the beginning of time the ancient ones had decided it was time to share the gift of immortality with the mortals. They placed the spirit of immortality deep within the mortals' beings, a place few would have the courage to explore.

"It was decided that at the time of each human's death an ancient one would come to answer any questions and to guide them home. The humans misunderstood this being and called him the Grim Reaper. Most humans feared his approach; they would quake in terror. Few understood the message of love and freedom this being brought. If they were willing to listen with their hearts, they could learn all the secrets of the universe. They could free themselves from the wheel of karma and take their place with the other light workers.

"Over the millennium, few humans availed themselves of this opportunity. Death could not force the person to listen; he could only share and hope the person would hear. It saddened him greatly when the person would not listen. His gift was precious and offered freely. The only thing people had to do was surrender their old beliefs and open themselves up to the truth. They had to decide to let the love in. Death could not force them to feel safe.

"If people were willing to listen, Death would tell them that they had always been safe, that nothing in the universe had the power to hurt them unless they gave it the power. He would tell them how they could be free of fear and feel only love. He would talk about the freedom that surrender allowed a spirit to experience and how control would dampen its powers.

"Death would talk about seeing the face of God within. . ."

The dying man began to cough violently. When his coughing subsided he said, "Why do you bother me with this foolishness, old man? Leave me alone so I can die in peace. I don't want to hear your drivel any longer." He looked and noticed his visitor had left.

The ancient one smiled. He had sat with this spirit many times before, each time hoping that the spirit would hear the truth. At least this time he had been able to see him for a short time. The man was still unable to hear the truth; maybe in his next life he would sit still long enough to listen.

The dictionary defines meditation as thinking in a contemplative manner. I have heard prayer described as talking to the universe and meditation as listening for the answers. Meditation on a daily basis is a requirement for anyone who truly wants to know themselves.

For years I was a seeker. I was constantly searching for the right teachers, books, classes or simply looking for the right answers. The one thing I avoided was being quiet; I religiously avoided anything that would allow me to look within myself. I was terrified at the thought of looking deep within, afraid of what I might or might not find. I was certain that if others

23

really knew who I was, they would hate me, and why would I want to spend any time alone with myself?

For years my life was based on a feeling that there was something wrong with me; that was why I kept looking for the answers outside myself. I was convinced that any answers I came up with were wrong; after all, what did I know? As I learned to love myself, I actually enjoyed being alone. I now love the time I spend meditating because it taught me this lesson.

Throughout this book we will be using many types of meditations. In this chapter, we will explore a few of the basic ways to meditate. Meditation is an extremely important tool. Without it, the only way to achieve the necessary states of consciousness for these explorations would be with the use of drugs such as peyote or mescaline. When drugs are used, we have no way of reproducing the same results each time, and we are limited to the use of drugs. There is also a chance of damaging our bodies and minds with the drugs. With meditation, there are no risks, and the outcome is much more predictable.

In order to explore these other realities, we must be able to go beyond our everyday waking consciousness and achieve an altered state of consciousness. Meditation is a wonderful technique that you can use to alter your consciousness as well as improve your state of mind and health. When we meditate, we quiet the mind, and we are then able to go beyond our everyday reality. As you enter that altered state of consciousness, you are open enough to experience the ethereal realms.

I always suggest meditation to my clients. So many of them resist the idea of doing it on a regular basis. I find most people dislike the idea of discipline and resist sitting still for fifteen minutes. One of the usual excuses is that they are too busy. I can assure you that one of the most nurturing things I ever did for myself was to get into the regular habit of meditating. It is such a restful and centering habit. When I meditate, I seem to have more time.

There are hundreds of meditations. Many religious or spiritual sects practice some form of meditation on a regular basis. There is no right or wrong way to meditate; each variation has its merit. The most important point is to remain open and flexible and to find a way that works for you. Do not judge your meditations or any of your process.

Dogma in any form only serves in helping us to remain stuck. I have found that the form of my meditations changes frequently. At times I use open-eye meditations, and at other times I become quiet and seem to drift away. Sometimes I feel I am busy thinking or obsessing about something during the meditation. Occasionally, I spend the time gathering information. I have learned to remain flexible and allow my meditations to change, to be whatever they are on any given day.

You will be using a variety of meditations designed for specific purposes. Until you become familiar with them, I suggest you use them as they are described. After you become comfortable with the meditations, you can change them, thus allowing them to evolve and become more personal. Make them your own. Each type of meditation is useful for a particular purpose and is not meant to be the only way. Experiment with them and see which ones feel the best. Allow your meditations to evolve and change; try to avoid judging or trying to control them.

As you proceed on this path you will find that both discipline and meditation are extremely useful and necessary behaviors to cultivate. Without either discipline or meditation, it will be difficult to achieve the results you want with this book or in your life in general. A good way to begin exploring both of these concepts might be to discipline yourself to begin meditating on a daily basis if you don't already.

Whenever I used to hear the word "discipline," I had the image of a nasty first-grade teacher wagging her finger at me, telling me that I was a bad girl. I had told myself that I was a free spirit, and that I didn't need discipline. I now find that having discipline in my life is freeing rather then constricting. I no longer have to have a debate with myself about what I am going to do. I know. I have used discipline to create useful routines in my daily life such as meditating and writing in my journal.

Remember that your experience of life is predominantly controlled by your definitions. If you have an aversion or negative reaction toward the idea of discipline you may want to redefine the concept for yourself. I have found that it is usually our definitions of a concept that create our resistance and seldom the concept itself. The easiest solution is to change your definitions. Whenever you have resistance to an idea, look at your perspective on the issue and the definitions you are using. What are you telling yourself about the issue? What are you saying mentally that causes the resistance? Often your resistance will crumble as you broaden your definitions.

Part of me believes that sleeping late is a wonderful luxury. Part of me knows the importance of getting up early in the morning so that I have time to meditate. Now my morning ritual has become so important to me that I always give myself plenty of time in the morning to complete it. When I don't, my day usually goes poorly. I feel like I spend the whole day playing catch-up. This awareness allowed me to redefine the relative importance of sleeping late.

At times my meditations have become uncomfortable because a lot of old emotions rose to the surface of my consciousness. Once I learned to acknowledge them and let them flow through me, I was free of them. In addition to the emotional benefits, the health benefits of meditation have also been well documented. Meditating for twenty minutes is much more restful than several hours of sleep. As we go into an altered state of consciousness, our bodies begin to produce hormones that alleviate stress and allow our bodies to repair themselves. It also allows our minds to become quiet enough to get out of themselves. Self-forgetting is a wonderful state of mind, both relaxing and peaceful.

CREATING A RITUAL

Meditation is easier when you set the stage for it. I found it easier to meditate after I created a ritual for myself. Years ago when I had insomnia a doctor suggested I create a bedtime ritual so that my mind would know it was time to go to sleep. I would do a series of behaviors such as brushing my teeth, taking a bath, and reading for a few minutes. Then I would go to bed and fall asleep easily. The ritual reminded me that it was time to sleep. The doctor also told me to only use the bed for sleeping, not as a place to read or eat. My insomnia was cured.

When I began to have trouble meditating, I used the same formula. I began meditating in the same chair. Before I sat down I would light a candle, put on soft music, and say a prayer. Then I would sit down and begin to focus my attention.

I suggest you create a ritual for yourself before you begin meditating. It can be as simple as sitting in the same place each time, playing mellow music, or lighting a candle. Do whatever seems appropriate to you; just be consistent.

When you first begin meditating, it takes discipline and concentration. After you are able to quiet your mind and let go, the effort is well worth it. Results, however, are immediate. As soon as you begin sitting in meditation for a few minutes, even if your mind is still racing, you do get results. Just continue with your practice. Don't be discouraged; sometimes it takes years of practice to completely quiet your mind. It may seem like a lot of work at first, but it is a wonderful gift and a necessary tool on your spiritual quest.

I find it useful to sit up straight either in a comfortable chair or against a wall or bed so I have something to lean against. It is best to find a time and place where you won't be disturbed for at least twenty minutes. Make sure you ask people not to disturb you and unplug the phone. I find it very jarring to be suddenly returned to normal consciousness, and if I am on the alert for someone's approach or the phone ringing, I find it much more difficult to relax.

After you have decided on a time and place, sit down and mentally give yourself permission to relax. Give yourself a few minutes to get settled and comfortable. If you feel the need to move during your meditation, do so. In one of my first meditation sessions, my nose started itching. I was afraid that if I moved I would "ruin" the meditation, so I suffered through the whole thing. When I told a friend of mine about it, she laughed and told me it was far better to scratch my nose than suffer.

Once you are comfortable, hold your head level and then gently look toward the ceiling. When your eyes begin to get tired, gently allow them to close. Physiologically, whenever you look up in this way, your mind automatically begins to emit alpha brain waves. As you relax, your mind shifts gears and your brain waves begin to change. When you are in a normal state of consciousness, your mind emits mainly beta brain waves. Alpha brain waves are a signal that you are entering an altered state of consciousness.

As you slowly settle down, you will feel a subtle shift in your brain, almost like a car shifting gears. Remain quiet and you will eventually notice it. To me it feels like a subtle click, as if my brain has suddenly relaxed. You will continue to have thoughts; you may become more aware of how many thoughts you actually have. At first it often feels like your mind is chattering endlessly. Try not to judge it. I find it helpful to view my thoughts as trains that are pulling into a station. I have a choice: I can remain at the station and watch my thoughts go by or I can jump on them and go for a ride.

Next begin to focus your attention on your breathing. Gently watch your breath as it moves effortlessly in and out of your body. Remind yourself that it is alright for your mind to relax; give yourself permission to do so. As you inhale, imagine you are breathing in relaxation. As you exhale, release anything unlike relaxation.

Ideally, when you meditate, you want to allow your thoughts to flow by without following them. Part of the discipline in meditation is to be vigilant and remember to pull yourself back to center. Whenever you find yourself somewhere off in thought, gently pull your attention back to your breathing. Center yourself again and watch the thoughts go by.

Be gentle with yourself. If you are harsh and judgmental, it only makes the process more difficult and less enjoyable. There is really no such thing as a wrong way to meditate, or a wrong way to do anything for that matter, so honor your process.

The purpose of meditating is to relax and nurture yourself. If you are judging the process, it certainly isn't relaxing. Be gentle with yourself. When I first learned to meditate, I took a transcendental meditation class. The instructors would have the students come in every so often to be "checked." They would have us sit quietly and meditate for a few minutes, and then they would ask a series of questions. No matter what our answers were, their reply was to nod their heads and say, "That is good." I was extremely frustrated. I wanted answers; I wanted an honest critique of my meditations; I wanted a grade. Now I have come to realize that anything you do in a meditation is good.

After you focus on your breathing for a few minutes, slowly begin to relax your body. Start either at your head or feet and focus on various parts of your body, relaxing them. If you start at your head, begin by focusing on your scalp. Become aware of all the muscles in your scalp and then relax each of them. Next become aware of the muscles around your eyes and feel them relax. Pay special attention to relaxing your jaw muscles; we often carry a lot of tension there. Allow your jaw to part slightly and let your tongue fall to the floor of your mouth.

Slowly go up and down your entire body and relax all of your muscles. Allow your chest to really open up, and begin breathing deeply so you can open your heart area. It feels so good when you completely relax your chest area. After you have relaxed your entire body, again focus on your breathing and allow your consciousness to drift.

At first I found myself frequently peeking at the clock but eventually I knew when the twenty minutes were up. At first that time seemed like a lifetime; I had a hard time making myself sit still for that long. Now I occasionally find myself meditating for longer and not minding at all.

Always give yourself a few minutes to come out of your meditation. Gently open your eyes and focus on the room, allowing yourself time to adjust to this reality. Avoid getting up suddenly or you may find yourself getting dizzy; your blood pressure does lower during a meditation.

I find it useful to meditate twice a day—shortly after I get up in the morning and before I go to bed at night. Try to find a time of day that you can consistently meditate and discipline yourself to do it each day. Once it becomes a habit you will wonder how you ever lived without it.

OPEN-EYE MEDITATION

Another form of meditation is with open eyes. First choose an object to focus on: candles, flowers, or water are good items to start with. Then get comfortable and focus your attention softly on your breathing. Begin by gazing gently at the object. Avoid looking directly at the item; gaze at it with your eyes barely open and slightly out of focus or look just beyond it. With your eyes open, relax your entire body and allow yourself to become one with the object. You could imagine yourself getting very tiny and walking around on the object. Mentally turn it around in your mind. Let the object talk to you. Allow your consciousness to merge with the object and relax. After twenty minutes, slowly bring yourself back to waking consciousness.

There are an infinite number of ways to meditate; these are only two. Practice them until you become proficient. Allow your meditations to evolve and change. As much as possible, relax and enjoy the process.

EXERCISES

1. Write about your definitions and beliefs of some of the key words in your reality. Start with the following words that are pivotal in your experience of reality, and then add your own:

spirituality

discipline

commitment

success

failure

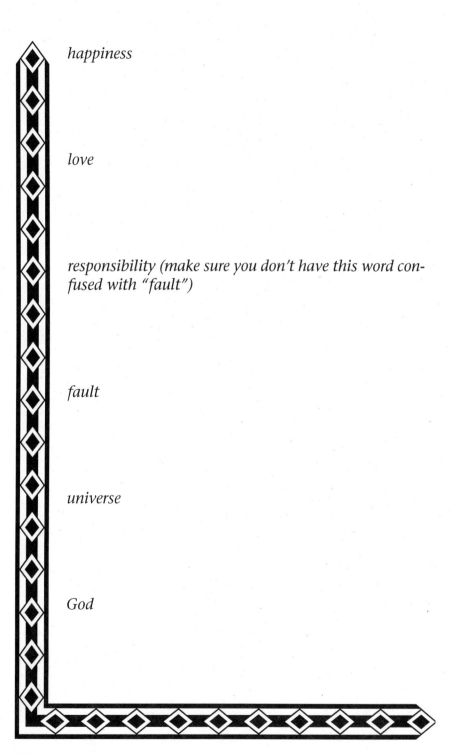

happiness

love

responsibility (make sure you don't have this word confused with "fault")

fault

universe

God

religion

authority

power

powerless

victim

Our reality is created by these definitions; make sure yours are not limiting your life. Look up the synonyms of these words as well. See if you have any of them confused with similar but limiting concepts. Free associate with these words and see what sort of emotions come up for you.

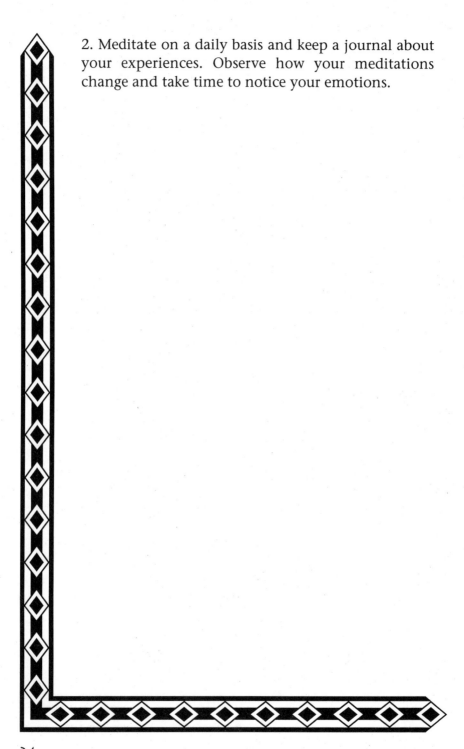

2. Meditate on a daily basis and keep a journal about your experiences. Observe how your meditations change and take time to notice your emotions.

3. Notice what you tell yourself about the issues in your life. Begin to observe your internal dialog and as much as possible, try to be objective. Spend time writing down those thoughts. Review them and begin to observe how your thinking limits you.

4. Begin to notice your dreams and write them down each morning. If you have a problem remembering them, before you go to sleep, affirm to yourself that you will remember your dreams and understand them. If that doesn't work, drink several glasses of water before you go to bed. When you get up to go to the bathroom, write down your dreams.

NOTES

▲▲▲ CHAPTER THREE ▲▲▲

MEETING YOUR PROTECTOR

Long ago the ancient ones stood in the swirling mists before time. They wanted to know more about who they were; they asked and the mists began to part. Slowly the universe emerged. The ancient ones looked upon this creation with love. There were millions of stars and planets. Each one was more magnificent than the next. The wind of creation raced through the universe, whispering and asking, but there was no one to hear.

They decided to create a special world in each galaxy. Each one was totally unique, and everything within it was created in a special manner to honor its uniqueness. Some of the planets were filled with magnificent crystal structures. Others were filled with water and land. Some were swirling masses of vapors that continued to recreate themselves.

The ancient ones were saddened because the universe was vast and beautiful, but also empty. There were no beings to enjoy its magnificence. One of the planets was very special to them. They filled its land with trees, plants, and flowers with wonderful scents and vibrant colors. They also created magical things like babbling brooks, mountains, rainbows, and waterfalls. They set the wind free upon this planet to softly caress the world and whisper the secrets of the universe, but still there was no one to hear its secrets.

Next they created animals of all shapes and sizes. They filled the ocean with fish, whales, and dolphins of all colors. The ancient ones looked upon their creation, and they were pleased, but there was still something missing. They decided to try an experiment on this wonderful planet and create beings in their own likeness. They gave the species called humans spirits just like their own; they placed the spirit within each individual's being in hopes that they would find it. The ancients then gave them the power to create and the freedom of choice, and hoped they would use these gifts wisely.

The wise ones knew that these spirits would eventually get restless and wish to return home. Since they created the world in love, it reflected their harmony and grace. All the systems were perfectly balanced and harmonious. The needs of all the creatures were easily met and the world was a safe and loving place to exist. All the creatures felt the love of their creator and knew they were safe. There was no fear.

The old ones gave humans the ability to see the truth in all things and to be aware of spiritual beings that were with them throughout their lives to guide and protect them. As the humans were born, they were each given a spiritual entity to guard them and to help them remember the truth while they existed on the earth plane. These beings loved them as much as life itself; they waited patiently for the humans to ask them for the help. They would never intrude upon the person's free will, but they were delighted when they were finally asked to help.

As time went by, the humans moved further and further away from their connection with their Creators. The old ones were saddened by this but they knew eventually the spirits would have to find their way home. The protectors were at the edge of their reality, just waiting for the people to reach out and ask for help. The love was always waiting, always there. The further people moved away from their spiritual centers, the more painful their existence became.

Eventually when the pain became intense enough, people would ask, "Who am I, and why am I here?" And at that moment they could reach out and a wonderful being of light would be there waiting, ready to guide and protect them as they began their journey home. The journey toward love.

We live in a universe that is completely safe and filled with love, yet most of the time we walk around in fear. As soon as we step into fear we cut off our connection to the love. We can no longer feel or access it. Energetically, fear makes us small. In order to remember our magnificence we must let go of the fear; we must move beyond it.

As you begin to explore the ethereal realms, it can be an exhilarating as well as a terrifying experience. These worlds are as real as ours although it often doesn't seem that way. These worlds frequently operate differently from our own. I learned the hard way to use caution and prudence when playing in those universes.

At the beginning of my studies, Miguel introduced me to a spiritual being he called my protector. At first I was confused and bothered by the idea of having or needing a protector, but I grew to appreciate his presence in my life. I have come to realize that we all have many beings of light on the ethereal level that are more than willing and able to help us in a variety of ways. Since I have become accustomed to their presence in my life, when I temporarily lose my connection with these beings, I feel like I am walking around without my favorite scarf wrapped around my neck.

These entities are already there for us; it is merely a matter of becoming aware of them, connecting with them, and asking them to help us. We were given free will by our Creator, therefore these beings will only assist us if we ask for their help. They will never knock on your door and ask if you need assistance, but the moment you give them permission to help you they are there. Our minds or egos can be rather stuffy at times. They seem to prefer ignoring all the help that is available to them. My mind would much rather do things its own way, even if the results are less than desirable.

When I first began delving into spirituality and psychic phenomenon, I often heard people talking about spirit guides and teachers. My mind painted a rather humorous and erroneous picture of the concept. I had an image of people sitting around in the clouds, smoking cigars, and playing an unusual game called Torment the Humans. They would alternately help, hinder, and then test us on our progress. If we hadn't "gotten it" yet, we would have to pay the price emotionally. Many people feel the same way about God because God is often portrayed by many religions as a judgmental being. Nothing could be further from the truth.

These beings are very loving energies. They never test or torment us in any way. They exist to assist and show us the easier, softer way to do things. We have to be willing to listen and act accordingly. Any feelings we have of emotional pain or being tested come from our resistance to change, not from their guidance. They often appear to us as humans or in the form of animals. They are not really Indian chiefs or Egyptian pharaohs or unicorns. They are actually an energy form, but those images seem easier for our minds to grasp and understand. Our minds seem to feel more comfortable when they have something to hold onto. My mind would rather believe it is "talking" to an Indian chief than admit it is getting rather interesting information from an energy form or an inorganic entity.

Each of these beings serves a different purpose. Our protector is mainly for our protection. Another being's main focus may be to guide us through a certain area of our life or to teach us. A certain entity may guide us through a particularly difficult relationship and then leave, while another entity may stay with us throughout our entire lifetime. Some of these entities are guides while others are teachers; they all have their own particular area of expertise and way of operating. Some people believe we have a specific number of teachers and guides.

Connecting with and using these energies certainly makes the journey toward our sacred centers a much easier and more joyous one. They are there to help us go beyond our limiting beliefs and experience of separation. They appear to be outside us or separate because we believe that we are separate. In truth we are all one; we really are those beings, and they merely mirror our inner beliefs. They serve a purpose in our lives as one of the many guideposts that are available to lead us home to our spiritual center.

THE POWER OF CEREMONIES

In this chapter you will connect with the energy that is called your protector. This energy is with you specifically to protect you from energies you may encounter in the other universes. Its purpose is to assist you in going beyond your fears. I find it a helpful energy to call upon whenever I am feeling unsafe or frightened. In order to connect with this entity, it is helpful to do a ceremony.

Ceremonies will play an important role in many of the exercises in this book. Ceremony can be a valuable and important tool. Centuries ago they were an integral part of everyday life; unfortunately we have moved away from the use of ceremonies. Many people judge ceremonies as being foolish or ignorant, but in fact, we can use them as a tool to assist us in going beyond the limitations of our rational, linear mind.

Ceremonies are a door to the ethereal, a simple way that we can call upon the forces of nature and the universe and ask for their assistance and guidance. We can use ceremonies to disengage our minds and to create magic in our lives. They can be wonderfully centering and empowering experiences.

A ceremony is an act of power. It is a series of actions in which we use our focus or intention to call upon energies beyond our normal perception. It can be any series of actions. We can use ceremony to make even mundane actions like brushing your teeth sacred. Anything can become a ceremony if that is your intention.

Ceremonies and rituals are similar. I think of a ritual as a ceremony that is repeated in the same fashion over and over again without thought. The Catholic Mass is an excellent example of a beautiful ritual. For centuries priests have performed the same acts over and over again. Unfortunately when a ceremony becomes a ritual, the participants often lose their focus or forget their intention. Without that focus the ritual becomes less meaningful. Much of the power is lost when a ceremony becomes simply ritual.

The main elements of a ceremony are the focus and the intention. With these two elements we create a bridge to the ethereal—in a sense we open a door to the other realms. Whenever I perform a ceremony, I first focus my mind on what it is I am about to do. Then I get very clear about what I want to create, and how I want to use the energy. I ask myself what the purpose of this ceremony is—what my intention is. Your intention is extremely important especially while exploring the ethereal realms. It is important to create intentions that are harmless and loving.

The next step in creating a ceremony is to decide on its form, how it will look. Some of the questions I ask myself are: Where would it be best to hold the ceremony? Is it necessary to be outside in the elements or inside? How many people are necessary? What objects will I need?

A ceremony can be as elaborate or as simple as you wish. Before I do a ceremony I become quiet, go within, and see what feels right. When I return to normal consciousness, I intuitively know what the ceremony will look like and what I need in order to perform it. Learning to do that is a matter of practice and of trusting your process. At first I was always sure I was wrong; now I know that whatever I do is perfect for that moment.

Once you have decided what you are going to do and have the stage set, you are ready to perform the ceremony. A ceremony is a sacred act; start with a simple prayer asking for guidance and assistance. Release as much of your ego as possible and begin to focus on your sacred center. Then allow yourself to get quiet and begin to center yourself. Focusing on your breathing will assist you in silencing your mind. Breathe deeply and rhythmically. Slowly, as your mind quiets, you can begin to step into that sacred center. Allow the power within you to build slowly and then begin the ceremony. After completing the ceremony, offer a prayer of thanksgiving and closing.

Since ceremonies are sacred acts, it is important that your intentions are clear and loving. Power is a seductive force. It is easy to be seduced into using power for selfish ends and to harm yourself and others in the process. Whenever you do a ceremony or use power in any way, focus your intention on being loving and harmless.

I will lead you in a variety of ceremonies. Once you become familiar with the various elements, feel free to adapt and change the ceremonies however you feel guided. Just make sure you are clear about your focus and intentions.

Any of the ceremonies can be done in a group or alone. Doing them in a group is more powerful than doing them alone, but a sacred act is always honored by the universe. The energy of a group tends to build exponentially, so rather than it being one plus one it is more like two times two. It is much better to do them alone than to not do them at all or to do them with someone who may mock the process.

One person usually acts as a guide or facilitator while the other people participate. All the ceremonies are written for use by a group. If you are doing a ceremony alone, I suggest you record the prayers and instructions so you can relax and enjoy the process.

The locations you choose for the ceremony will be up to you. It is important to find the perfect location. For some of the ceremonies I may suggest doing them indoors, but find a spot that feels right to you, a place of power, a place that feels sacred and safe. To do this, relax and quiet your mind. Breathe deeply and quietly ask yourself which location would be the best place to hold this ceremony. Notice any mental images or impressions that you receive. These promptings tend to be subtle so ask gently of yourself, and most importantly be patient. Do you see yourself near a brook? Do you see trees and rocks around you or do you see yourself in your bedroom? Remain relaxed and observant, don't try to force yourself. If you are patient and remain relaxed, the answer will always come.

I think of these promptings as a gentle wind that blows softly around the edge of my consciousness. You must train yourself to notice these subtle energies. In the course of a normal day the temperature around you probably varies quite a bit, but you never notice it unless the change is drastic. If you really concentrated, you could become sensitive to subtle variations in the temperature. It is the same way with the energies around us. It is a matter of patiently practicing. Later, you will be doing exercises specifically designed to increase that sensitivity.

Have you ever noticed how people frequently sit in the same place? Each time they enter a room they head for their favorite spot. Intuitively, they have picked out a place of power for themselves in that room. Have you ever walked into a familiar room and found someone sitting in your spot? How did it feel? Some of that behavior is habit, but how did you pick the spot in the first place? Begin to notice how you choose.

MEETING YOUR PROTECTOR

Meeting your protector is a private act, so this ceremony requires a place away from the group as well as a place for the group to sit in meditation. I usually do this ceremony indoors. The recipients sit in the meeting room while the leader waits in a place off to the side that is private.

When I do this ceremony for my students, I have everyone stand in a circle in the meeting room while I do the opening prayer. Then I have them sit down with their backs straight and go into a meditative state. I tell them to focus on their intentions and ask the universe for guidance and assistance. I retreat to the other room and go into a light trance. I instruct each of them to enter the other room one by one whenever it seems appropriate, in whatever order seems right.

As each person enters, I say a short prayer and ask the universe to assist me in introducing these two energies. I then ask the person's protector to reveal itself. I introduce the protector by name and give the person a few minutes to become accustomed to its presence. Then I give thanks and the person leaves. After everyone has received their protector, I return to the meeting room and say a closing prayer.

We then talk about the experience. It is extremely important to write or talk about these experiences because it grounds them in this reality. Your mind is not accustomed to accessing information from the ethereal level. By acknowledging it in some way, your mind will begin to realize that it is okay to notice those energies.

Your protector is a loving and kind energy. Its sole purpose is to protect you. As with anything, it takes time to develop a relationship with this energy. When I call upon my protector, I feel as if the universe has just wrapped a warm blanket around my shoulders. Whenever I am going through a particularly stressful time, I call upon this energy, and I feel safer. It is important to call upon this energy whenever you go into a meditation or explore any of the ethereal realms. This energy will help keep you safe and protect you from harm if you remember to ask it to do so.

After you do this ceremony, spend some time adjusting to its presence. Call upon it and then open yourself up so you can feel its presence. Become familiar with how it feels and how it touches you. You may begin to perceive it as a person and feel its presence during your day.

I generally light a candle before I start the ceremony and burn sage to cleanse the area. Then I quiet my mind, breathe deeply, focus my intention, and step into my center of power. I open with a prayer such as:

Great Spirit, Universe, Creator, we humbly ask for your love and your guidance. We ask that your power fill this sacred place with your love. May you guide all of us

*this day as we come before you. Bless us and allow us to be
harmless always.*

*We call upon the six directions: north, south, east,
west, up, and down. May we be surrounded by your protection. We call upon the powers of the universe: earth,
wind, water, and fire. May your power give us strength and
wisdom.*

*We humbly come before you this day to meet our lov-
ing protectors so they may guide us on our journeys. We
wish to know you and ourselves better. We seek the path
that will lead us home to you. Please guide us and bless us.
May only beings of light enter this place, and may we be
divinely guided.*

We come in love and light. And we give thanks.

The facilitator then retreats into the other room and goes
into a deep meditative state, sitting on the floor in a cross-
legged position.

INSTRUCTIONS FOR FACILITATOR

As the meditators come into the room, have them sit quietly in
front of you, gaze at them softly through barely open eyes, and
gently take their hands in yours. Relax and begin to breathe
deeply and in harmony with the person in front of you. Then
mentally ask the universe for assistance. Relax and trust the
process. Close your eyes and allow your mind to settle down.
Then say:

*Universe, we come before you this day to introduce
this person to his or her loving protector. We ask this
energy to make itself known to us now.*

Take a few deep breaths and allow the energy to build. Feel the presence of this entity and welcome it. Ask if it is willing to reveal its name to you. At this point a name will usually pop into your mind and often some information about the energy. Trust the process, relax, and remain open. Don't strain; let the answers come. If you don't clearly hear the name, it will usually come to the person shortly either in a meditation, dream, or as an impression. Give the person a few minutes to become accustomed to this energy, then give thanks to the universe and allow the person to leave.

When everyone has received a protector, have someone change places with you and repeat the procedure. There is no way you can fail with this exercise because everyone already has a protector, they simply aren't consciously aware of it. As with any of the exercises, practice and patience are the key ingredients. If someone doesn't feel a protector right away, have him or her call upon it on a regular basis and eventually it will happen.

Have everyone sit in the room and offer a closing prayer:

> *Great Spirit, Universe, Creator, we give thanks for your love and your guidance. We ask that you bless each of us as we go out from this place. We give thanks that we are one step closer to knowing you and returning home. Show us how to make all of life sacred.*
> *We come in love and light and we give thanks.*

Now have everyone share their experience. If you are doing this alone, write about it in your journal. Allow each of your experiences to be yours and yours alone. Don't compare yourself to other people. Each person has a unique path; much like a fingerprint, no two are alike. Honor your process and know that it is special. It is not better or less than another person's. It is yours and yours alone. Honor it for its uniqueness and beauty.

EXERCISES

1. Spend time in meditation each day with your protector. Begin to explore your relationship. Allow it to deepen and unfold. Relax and enjoy it. Write about your experience here:

2. Keep a journal about your experiences. Are you beginning to "go places" in your meditations? How are you feeling? What, if anything, is changing in your life?

3. Begin to write your personal myth. Write about your life as if you are a fictional character on an odyssey like Ulysses. Where is fate taking you? Do you slay the dragon or make it your friend? Do you even see the dragon? Does your story have a happy ending? Let your imagination run wild. Give yourself a few hours to sit and write. Let the story flow from you. It is amazing what this process can reveal to you about yourself. Your myth will change as your process continues to unfold.

NOTES

▲▲▲ Chapter Four ▲▲▲

GROUP MEDITATIONS

The late afternoon sun was shining weakly in the winter sky. The air had a deep chill, and she knew it was going to be a cold night. The old woman sat next to her hearth, waiting. Her room always smelled inviting. No one ever saw her cook, yet she always had treats for her visitors. The children would arrive soon, and she smiled as she drifted off to sleep. Her naps were growing longer with each passing year; soon she would return home to the ancient ones.

When she again opened her eyes the children were sitting quietly at her feet, waiting. She loved this time of day. The sun was just above the horizon and all the cooking fires in the village were blazing. The aromas made her mouth water. The children's faces beamed with excitement as she greeted each one by name. Oh how she loved the little ones. The thought of leaving them saddened her; however, that time hadn't arrived yet.

One brave little soul looked up and asked her to tell them the story about the wolf. For what seemed like centuries, she had been teaching the little ones with her stories. Each day they gathered in her room to hear her. When the men who had come from other villages began to grumble about her being a witch, the ones who had sat at her feet would silence them. The women would be quick to remind them that the children received only love and valuable lessons about life from her.

She took a deep breath and in her warm and resonant voice said, "So you want to hear about the wolf? Who here remembers the story?" Only the very young ones failed to raise their hands. She reached into her pockets and pulled out treats. As the children passed them around, she began her story.

"During the darkest part of the winter long ago, a lonely wolf came into the village. The warriors ran for their weapons, but before they had the chance to hurt the wolf, a little girl walked over to the animal and noticed that his paw was injured. She reached out to hug the wolf and told the warriors to move away. She did so with such power that they all obeyed.

"She gently led the wolf into her dwelling and bathed his wound. He looked at her with eyes filled with wisdom and fell into a deep sleep as she cleaned his wounds. When he awoke many hours later she had cooked him a bowl of broth filled with the little bit of meat she had left. He gratefully accepted her gift and when he was done, he again fell asleep.

"The little girl laid down next to the wolf and went to sleep. His fur next to her was comforting and she quickly fell into a deep sleep. She found herself standing before the ancient ones, the wolf beside her. She felt humble and small.

"The old one smiled gently down at her and said, 'We are very proud of you, little one. You reached out in love to another being, one who needed your help. You saved this being's life. Mankind has too long worked alone. They have come to believe that they are superior to the other animals they walk among. You are all one, my children.'

"For years the little girl had felt this way. Hearing the truth gave her the courage to speak to this old one. She said, 'But when I try to tell the others that the animals talk to me, they laugh. The hunters give thanks to the spirits of those they kill but they still kill them. They do not ask the animal first if it wants to die.'

"The old ones nodded their heads and said, 'That is why you are here, little one. You are here to take a message back to your elders and they will listen this time. The children are a special gift given to the humans. When humans are young they can communicate with all creatures. From this day forth, you shall teach with your stories. You will remind others that life is meant to be lived in harmony with all beings and creatures. You must teach others to treat everyone and everything with dignity and respect. Mankind must learn to act only in love, never with anger, hate, or greed. People must work together, in that way they will again find their way home.'

"'But how will I get the people to listen, wise one?' asked the girl.

"'Trust me, little one, the story of how you tamed the wolf is already spreading. The wolf is a feared creature, yet you healed him and saved his life. You sleep beside him with no fear for your own safety. The people now know you are special.'

"When she awoke in the morning she could hear people talking outside her room. As she stepped out of her dwelling place, the wolf stood beside her and a murmur went through the crowd. His fur was snow white and it glistened in the sunlight. She hugged him lovingly and then in a voice much stronger than her years should have allowed, she told her people of the dream."

The old woman's eyes again focused on the room and the children could hear their mothers calling them to dinner. "What happened next, Grandmother?" asked one of the little ones. "Yes, what happened to them? You never tell us," said one of the older ones.

"Perhaps one day soon I will tell you the rest of the story, little ones. It is almost time to finish the stories anyway." The old lady smiled as the children scampered off to their dinners.

Soon, very soon, she thought to herself.

Children frequently have invisible playmates and often get lost listening to the whispers in the wind. I can remember ice skating as a child and seeing a leaf trapped beneath the ice. I laid down on the ice and got lost in the world beneath the surface. I was fascinated, but my parents were furious—they thought I had fallen and hurt myself. They had lost their sense of magic long ago.

As we grow older we are told directly or indirectly to grow up. We forget those feelings of oneness; we forget to talk to the animals. Part of finding your sacred center is learning how to listen again to those gentle whispers. It is time to reclaim your birthright. In order to do that, we must get quiet and go within.

Quietly sitting down alone and relaxing into a deep meditative state is a wonderful feeling, but meditating in a group can be a powerful and exhilarating experience. The larger the group, the more energy is available. You can harness that energy and use it for a variety of wonderful purposes.

This additional energy can be used for healing, emotional clearing, gaining information, traveling to other realities, or simply feeling better. The possibilities are endless. One of the main objectives of this path is to gain personal power. The easiest way to gain this power is by meditating in a group. As you gain personal power, the more centered you become and the easier it is to live from your sacred center.

You *must* get to know yourself. As this inner awareness expands, so will your personal power. As this power grows, you will have the necessary strength and courage to look clearly at your life. You will begin to see beyond the illusions of your ego and step more fully into your spiritual center. The more you free yourself of your ego, the clearer a channel you become for the love of the Creator. Then you can handle more power and use it to create joy and abundance in your life and in the lives of the people you care for.

As you become more familiar with handling power, you can direct the energy of the group, and you can also use it to assist in achieving your desired outcomes. The group's energy will help you collectively as well as in your individual healing. As the energy of the group grows, so does your own.

When you meditate in a group, it is important to have a leader or facilitator. This person is responsible for guarding the group, guiding and balancing the energies, as well as calling the group back at the end of the meditation. As you become familiar with the feeling of the group and of energy, the way to do this will become easier. It is something you *feel* rather than *think*. This topic will be discussed in detail later in the chapter.

I suggest doing most group meditations inside unless they are part of a specific ceremony. Animals are attracted by the energy generated during a meditation. It can be disconcerting to open your eyes and see a cow or strange dog staring at you.

There are an endless number of configurations that can be used with a group. Each variation creates a different energy pattern and therefore, a different result. The placement of the people (who sits where and what configuration the group sits in) has a profound effect on the experience of the individual participants. Knowing how to choose the layout for the meditation is something you learn through experience. Eventually you intuitively know which configuration to use and where people need to sit. It is part of the learning. You must each learn to trust and honor your own process, and this is a wonderful place to begin.

When I first began guiding group meditations, I was certain my choices were wrong, but I chose anyway. Today there are still times I doubt my choice, but I act as if it is right, and it always is. There are no errors in this universe. Our minds often choose to judge our choices as good or bad by the outcomes they achieve, but in truth there are only outcomes—period. Good and bad are merely a matter of perspective, a product of your mind's attempt to explain things and its need to be right. Trust your choices.

In this chapter, you will explore how to be a group leader, how to handle the energy of a group, and a number of configurations for group meditations. What follows is by no means a complete list of all the configurations that are available. Let your imagination and intuition be your guide.

THE MEDITATION LEADER

Much of what the leader does is intuitive in nature. That intuitive nature resides in our feminine aspect. Frequently that part of us has never been honored—learn to honor it now. I can explain the mechanics of the actions, but you will have to trust your own judgment. As you begin to lead meditations, don't second guess yourself or allow other people to; trust your choices. They are usually right, and if they aren't, you will get to choose again next time. Go more by how things feel rather than what you think they "should" be. Listen to your feminine self, listen for that still voice within you that knows only love.

The first thing the leader does is choose the configuration for the meditation. That is often dependent upon the number of people present or the results you hope to achieve. As I explain the various meditations, I will mention what they are most useful for. Consider those parameters, but ultimately let your intuition be your guide.

Once you have decided on the configuration, you will have to decide where to place the various participants. Often people will intuitively place themselves in the right position, but the leader has to balance the energy of the group as a whole. To do this, stand in the center of the group and take a few deep breaths. Begin to "see" the group in your mind's eye and mentally rearrange the people. Ask yourself where people need to be and let the answers come; the more you honor and trust your process, the easier this will become. As you place people, allow the picture to readjust itself as necessary. Feel free to change your mind and move people several times. The first time the group meets you could take turns being the leader. Move people around and notice how the room begins to feel different as everyone sits in a different location. You could have one person sit in the center with her eyes closed observing the sensations in the room as people move around.

Once a leader is chosen for a meditation, allow his or her choices to remain unquestioned. It is disruptive to a person's faith in his or her intuition if everyone adds their two cents. No one is right or wrong.

Once everyone is in place, begin the meditation. If possible, lower the lights and tell everyone to relax. Mentally call upon beings of light to protect and guide the group, call upon your protector, and then relax. Breathe deeply and begin to move around the group. Whenever you channel energy, you collect or gather the energy with your left hand and send it with your right hand. Hold your left hand up and use it like an antenna to gather the energy. Turn it until you feel that you have a secure connection with the energy, and then begin moving the energy around the group with your right hand. Usually the energy moves around the group counter-clockwise but as always, let your intuition guide you.

As you channel energy into the various participants you are helping them balance their energies. As you work in the various power points, you will also assist people in releasing some of the emotional garbage from the past that holds them back. Focusing the energy assists them in finding that sacred center and feeling the love.

Next, stand in front of each participant and scan them with your right hand. Stop wherever it seems necessary or appropriate and let energy flow into that place. Pay particular attention to the top of the person's head, around the heart and the upper back. There are power points located in these areas on the body. After you have circulated around the group, find a comfortable place to stand. With your feet spread shoulder-width, close your eyes and relax. Allow yourself to drift into a light meditative state. When the time seems right, call the group back by gently telling them it is time to come back. Check to make sure everyone is back. Have the group remain quiet until everyone is. After everyone has returned, warn them that the light is about to be turned on, then turn the lights up.

Occasionally, people will be so far out of their bodies that they will not come back immediately. Never touch them without warning; it can be very unsettling. Go over and gently tell them that it is time to come back, call their name and call again. If they still don't come back, tell them that you are going to touch them, and gently pick up their hands. Rub their wrists together; this will always bring them back. If others are disoriented after the meditation, having them rub their wrists together will help relieve the feeling.

Once everyone is back, it is useful to have people share their experiences. As I have said before, try not to judge your experience by other people's experiences. As always, honor your process. Remember that experiences are not good or bad, they are just different. Honor the differences instead of comparing them.

FLYING MEDITATION

The flying meditation is a type of group meditation for which you only need one other person, your partner. It is used mainly for emotional clearing and to acquaint yourself with alternate universes. It is a freeing and energizing form of meditation in which you will literally feel like you are flying. As with all meditations, first call upon the energy of your protector before you begin.

Find a comfortable place on the floor for you and your partner to sit. One person acts as a ground or guide and sits up while the other person lies down and "flies." As you can see in Figure 1, the person sitting up is erect with legs crossed. The person who is going to fly lies on his stomach with his head in the other person's lap. The person then stretches his arms out perpendicular from his body and gets as comfortable as possible. The person sitting up gently holds the "flyer's" head in his or her hands and they both begin to go into a light meditation.

As the guide, you will need to pay attention to all the details. Begin by mirroring the other person's breathing. Slowly allow your breathing patterns to synchronize; this will allow you to build rapport with the other person. As you do this, you will both begin to drift into a more relaxed state.

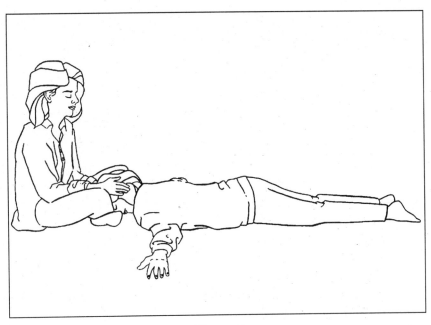

Figure 1

You may get a true sense of what is going on emotionally with the other person. Part of your function as the guide is to allow the other person's emotions to flow through you so that you can discharge them. Take care not to make them your own; simply allow them to flow through you without judgment. They are merely an energy that you easily release.

Shortly after you have both relaxed, you will begin to feel emotions rising in your body. You may suddenly become sad, angry, or feel like laughing, and you will wonder where the feelings are coming from. Remember that you are merely feeling the other person's emotions, and all you have to do is allow them to flow back into the earth. They will feel like your own emotions. The trick is to remain focused and send them down your spine and into the earth. You do not want to hold onto them in any way. It is not necessary to report to your partner what you were feeling.

As you continue to sit with your eyes closed, you may feel moved to allow your hands to hover over various parts of your partner's body. Allow yourself to do so and as always, let yourself be guided by your intuition. Some of the most powerful spots to work are around the chakras, the seven energy centers in the body, and below the right shoulder blade. These areas often work like switches and will propel the person into other realities or will cause them to release emotions or situations.

These meditations usually last for fifteen to twenty minutes. When you feel it is time to end the meditation, begin to gently stroke the person's head. Gently turn your partner's head to one side and begin to massage his or her ears, especially at the top of the ear and around the outer edge. The ears are filled with pressure points. Let your intuition guide you as you rub the tip and interior. Allow several minutes for both of you to come back to this reality. I have yet to do this mediation without both my feet going to sleep, so get up slowly.

The person who "flew" will often go through a wide variety of emotions and experiences. At first the mind chatter is intense. At some point most people become concerned about the other person's legs and are afraid that their head will be too heavy. As much as possible, allow these concerns to fade when you are the one "flying." As your mind becomes quiet, your chest will begin to feel heavy and you will notice the grounding effect of the earth. Emotions will seemingly come from nowhere and disappear just as quickly. You will begin to feel more calm and centered. You will find yourself drifting off into a deep meditative state.

Eventually you will feel as if your consciousness is slowly peeling up out of your body, as if you are slowly separating. At first you might find yourself slamming back into your body as soon as you notice this sensation, but with practice you will find yourself leaving your body and "flying." It is an exhilarating experience and at times can be frightening. Let yourself relax into the experience as much as possible.

This meditation does takes practice. It may take several sessions before you can leave your body and feel the full effects of it. It is an excellent choice if you are feeling particularly emotional or need to quiet your mind. Once you are able to fly, it is good to use if you want to gather specific information and a larger group isn't available.

TRIANGLE MEDITATION

This meditation has an almost endless number of variations. It is particularly useful for traveling to other realities and gaining information. The basic triangle mediation requires at least four people. One person acts as the guide while the other three sit on the floor in a triangular formation. The participants can sit with their knees touching. They may or may not hold hands. While I was studying with Miguel we would put a huge crystal in the center of the triangle. Later we would use it to focus on when we wanted to gather information. You could also use a candle to represent the ethereal flame within each of us.

Figure 2

The center of the triangle is powerful. If you need to gain extra power to access information, it is an excellent place to sit. All the energy seems to gather at the center of the triangle. People often sense a column of light emanating from the center of the triangle during this meditation.

The guide begins by moving the energy around the triangle and then guiding it up from the center of the group. After you feel that the energy is flowing freely, begin to work on the individuals. Then find a place to stand and relax, usually opposite one of the participants (Figure 2).

A powerful variation of this meditation takes at least seven people. Have three people sit facing inward in a triangle and three facing outward between them (Figure 3).

You can expand this meditation by also including a circle around the double triangle, or you can vary it by including a person in the center of the triangles. Yet another variation on

Figure 3

Figure 4

this meditation is to use a larger group of people. Have three people sit in the center in a triangle and then surround them with a circle or ring of protection often referred to as a ring of fire. You can have the people in the circle sit close enough to hold hands.

An interesting combination of these meditations requires six people. You can do a flying meditation in star or triangle formation (Figure 4). Have the people in the inner triangle sit facing outward with their backs touching. Have the other people lie in their laps and do a flying meditation. This configuration is extremely healing for all the participants.

CIRCLE MEDITATION

As the name implies, the configuration of this meditation is a circle. It is one of the simplest meditations to choreograph. Have each person sit in the circle. You can combine this meditation with any of the others.

As with all of the meditations, carefully place each of the participants. Intuitively balance the energy of the group, and once everyone is seated, begin the meditation. Circle around the group channeling energy. When the meditation is over, gently call the group back. This technique can be used as a generic meditation; it is good for relaxing, clearing, healing, and centering.

You can also do this meditation with a larger group and sit in groups of triangles, or arrange a central triangle with a circle around it. The people in the circle can do the same exercise or simply meditate (Figure 5).

ENERGY EXCHANGE MEDITATION

This meditation is not only fun, but also helps people begin to sense a wide variety of energies. It will assist you in becoming more sensitive to other people's energies as well as your own.

Figure 5

For this meditation you will need a partner or a group of people.

Sit cross-legged on the floor opposite one another about a foot apart. Get comfortable, close your eyes, and relax. Allow yourself to slowly drift into a meditative state. Then begin to project energy toward your partner from an area between your solar plexus and navel. You can do this by imagining a ribbon of energy leaving your body and entering your partner's body. You can create any number of mental images as long as they feel comfortable and effortless. At the same time open yourself up to receiving your partner's energy. Relax and breathe deeply.

Allow yourself to remain receptive and continue to send energy toward your partner. Continue the meditation for about fifteen minutes. When you are almost done, withdraw your energy from your partner and gently close the opening.

People describe a wide variety of experiences after they do this meditation. The first time I did it, I felt like I was in a gerbil tunnel going into my partner's abdomen. I felt tiny as I traveled through her entire body. Another woman said she went into her partner and then flew out of her head and into a field of stars. Often there are physical sensations in your body and on the skin in the stomach area. Sometimes you come back with knowledge about your partner's health and life that you didn't have before.

The variations on these meditations are endless. Use your intuition and imagination to explore the possibilities. Try using different geometric patterns and see how each one feels. I find that symmetrical patterns create more harmony and that the energy flows more easily. Experiment for yourself.

It is important to process the information you receive during these meditations. Your mind would much rather pretend that these other realities don't exist. Talking about your experiences helps release some of this denial. Always allow time for everyone to share their experiences at the end of the meditations. Accept your experience unconditionally; try to suspend judgment as much as possible as you explore this path. It will make the process more fun and less stressful.

EXERCISES

1. Keep a journal of your meditations. Review it weekly. Notice any trends or changes in your perspective or world view.

2. Make a commitment to yourself to meditate twice a day for at least a month, leading to a commitment for life. Begin to record your experiences here.

3. Experiment with each type of meditation. Experiment with yourself and other people. Record the results.

NOTES

CHAPTER FIVE

SACRED PLACES AND HELPERS

"But why?" asked the student.

"Because the ancient ones are omnipresent, they are never far away. We must always treat sacred places with care lest we forget the reason the ancient ones gave them to us," replied the teacher. "You must begin to act with reverence or you will hurt yourself or someone else. Acts of power are not that important—getting what you want doesn't really matter over time—but treating all of life as sacred is perhaps the most important thing you can do."

"But why would I be hurt or hurt someone else..."

"Why, why, why," interrupted the teacher. Once again he found himself getting impatient with this student's questions. He was beginning to wonder if he would ever understand anything other than his own sense of self. "Because 'y' is a crooked letter or because the answer to 'why' is 'why not.' How many times have I told you 'why' is a useless question? It is more important to understand *what* you can do or *how* you can change the results you are getting; 'why' merely gives you an excuse for doing what you have been doing. 'Why' allows you to stay the same. 'Why' is another way to try to prove yourself right and someone else wrong. Right and wrong are the mark of a person defending his mind." The teacher took a deep breath and got centered again.

"Let me tell you a story. Long ago the ancient ones stood upon the earth and they saw how hard mankind was struggling to find its way home. Men had lost sight of their sacred centers and relied totally on their brains and limited senses of self. The ancients wanted to help, but mankind had free will so they couldn't interfere—they could only help if people asked them for it. They loved the humans so much and it hurt to see them struggle so needlessly.

"Men had begun to walk the earth in fear. They even feared their old friend Death. They feared the shadows and Mother Nature. Most sad was the fact that they even feared one another. They had begun to practice elaborate rituals to find one they called God, an entity who seemed to live outside of themselves. Many had even lost hope. They had forgotten the importance of their spirits, and they listened not to the guidance of their unseen helpers.

"Humans had forgotten that their lives were a gift. That gift was freely given by the Creator, but it was a gift nonetheless. They had forgotten how to honor, truly honor, themselves, each other, the Earth Mother, and their Creator. They had lost the spark of true love that only lives in the absence of judgment. The old ones loved them and were saddened by their struggle.

"The old ones thought of many ways to help the human beings, but each was in turn rejected because it interfered in some way with their free will. Finally, one of the ancient ones suggested making places where the barrier between the spiritual realms and the physical realms was thinner. In that way the love of the spiritual world would become more accessible to any human who sought out that spot—if they chose to feel it.

"The old ones decided to create places where humans could feel the presence of their love whenever they chose. They created a few areas in the darkest places, and they were effective. Humans seemed drawn to them and felt empowered by being there. Once the humans aligned themselves to the energy of the place, they could use that power to create magic. But most importantly, the love helped some of them remember their own sacred natures. Some still focused on their own selfish ends, but the healing had begun. These power spots acted as reflectors so if a person came in love, the love came back multiplied; if they came in greed, their greed also came back to them.

"The old ones also decided to place a being of light at each location to act as a guardian, guide, and teacher. People could easily connect with them and ask for help. Slowly the humans who chose to use these places were able to release some of their fears. Unfortunately, the humans also began to believe that God had created these places, and they created legends and rituals to control their use.

"The old ones wanted everyone to have access to these places. They decided to give humans the ability to create them for themselves; whenever anyone acted in a sacred manner, asked for help, or gathered with others to search for the truth, a sacred place would be created—a place where their love could be felt.

"Although the ancient ones were happy about their solution, they thought it certainly had been easier when humans knew they moved in a sea of love and that they were gods themselves."

The teacher asked the student if there were any questions. He rolled his eyes in frustration when the first word out of the student's mouth was "why."

Finding the sacred place within ourselves is often a real struggle. Frequently my clients will tell me how safe and loved they feel in my presence. They will say, "You make me feel so good." I always remind them that they make themselves feel good, that I am only a mirror. But most people don't want to accept responsibility for their own creation. They prefer to pretend or believe that their good feelings come from "out there;" that they are in love *with* something, rather than admit they *are*

love. The love is always present, but we would rather pretend that it is coming from outside ourselves. We often get lost in our "whys" instead of looking at our choices. It would seem as though humans fear looking at themselves. We forget that we are pure love and that we are sacred.

Our lives were meant to be sacred. As you begin to exercise your choice to make life a sacred act, your life takes on a new dimension. The sacred self knows life is an illusion, but it understands fully how precious and sacred each moment is. When that sacred self lives in love, fear slips away and you become truly free. The sacred self has a reverence for everyone and everything. It has no need to judge anything or anyone. It is the essence of who and what you are.

The dictionary defines sacred as something or someone that is consecrated, dedicated, or devoted to a deity and as being revered. I think of sacred more in terms of how it makes me feel; in that way it is no longer a static definition. When I am in a sacred place or in touch with my sacred nature, I feel connected, centered, and solemnly, gently joyous. It is a wonderful and loving experience. I am at peace.

One day while I was living in California, I went to one of the old Spanish missions. As soon as I entered the chapel I was amazed by the energy in the church. It felt extremely peaceful and sacred. Even though I wasn't raised Catholic, I experienced a sense of connection whenever I entered the old mission. I would light a candle and meditate while I mentally released anything that was bothering me. As soon as I lit a candle, I felt as if I had released my cares. I was filled with a sense of reverence and peace as I sat there. For me, it was a sacred act.

For centuries people had entered that old mission to worship their concept of God. They had consecrated the building with their beliefs and acts of worship. The chapel became a sacred place because of the intentions of all the people who had entered the mission. Each person who lit a candle added to the power of those who came before them and those who would come after them.

Many of the older churches were built on places considered sacred by the indigenous peoples. In America churches
were often built on old burial sites or other locations sacred to
the Native Americans. In Europe, many of the churches were
built over ancient temple sites. Those sites were originally chosen because they were sacred places. Ancient people were more
in tune with the energy of the earth. Their spiritual leaders
always chose sacred places in which to worship. They lived in
harmony with nature and, therefore, were more sensitive to the
energies in various locations.

There are areas of land, specific positions on this planet,
that are inherently sacred. Sacred places can be thought of as
places of power or power spots. In a sense they are similar to a
person's chakras. They are areas where the barriers between our
universe and the ethereal realms are not as dense. A sacred
place can be thought of as a door to the ethereal, a doorway to
your own spirituality.

For eons, people have gone to sacred places to worship.
When the first individuals came upon a certain site, they felt its
inherent power. They were able to feel a greater concentration
of that energy; they felt loved. At first the people who came to
that place also felt the energy. Eventually, people went there
because it had become a tradition. Today, many frequently go
to church out of habit because that is how they believe they
have to worship God. They have forgotten the original reason
people went to sacred places—because it worked. It was easier
to connect with their spirit guides or their concept of God
when they were in those sacred locations.

Sacred places can be found all over the earth. You can also
learn how to create one easily for yourself by focusing your
intentions. Just as the millions of people who have worshipped
in a church make it a holy or sacred place, you can do the same
for yourself by deciding to create a sacred place. A sacred place
can be a powerful tool in your quest for peace of mind and in
connecting with your sacred self. Today, I enjoy sitting quietly
in a church or another sacred place meditating and connecting

with the universe and with my sacred center. I feel peaceful and loved.

The ancient Hawaiians worshipped and studied in a place called a *Heiau*. Most of them have long since been swallowed up by nature. Recently, I located an abandoned *Heiau* and took some of my students there. As soon as we approached the area, we could feel its power. The energy was huge and loving. We did a ceremony and the healings that took place were powerful. Everyone was deeply moved; there was hardly a dry eye in the group. The love we experienced was so gentle that it was almost overwhelming.

We can designate any place as sacred by simply saying it is and then acting as if it is. As we treat it in a sacred manner over time, it begins to feel more sacred. When we consecrate a location, we make it sacred. In a sense, we have opened a door to the ethereal and we have given the universe permission to channel more energy into that area. As we stand in that area and change our focus by performing a simple ceremony, we open the door and consecrate the location. We have created a sacred place.

When I go somewhere to teach or when I move into a new house, I do a simple ceremony to bless the place and make it sacred. It can be as simple as saying a prayer and calling upon the universe to bless it and make it holy. Often our minds want to make things more complicated than necessary, but it really is as simple as focusing our intentions and calling upon the universe for help.

CREATING AN ALTAR

Another powerful tool that can be helpful to you whenever you wish to focus your mind is an altar. Almost every temple or church contains an altar of some sort. An altar is a specific structure or location where ceremonies take place. You can find complicated instructions for creating an altar, but it is really a very simple process. You can use any type of material you wish to make your altar, in any shape or size. It can be wooden, such as a simple shelf, or it can be a piece of cloth that you use to symbolize an altar. Take as much time as you need to find just the right objects for your altar. Spend some time meditating about your altar—how would you like it to look? Will it be a permanent structure or something you can roll up and carry with you? What will you put on it? How will you use it?

Relax as you think about this process, let it be something that you enjoy fantasizing about. Relax and remember that there is no right or wrong way to make it. However you create your altar and whatever it looks like, it is yours and yours alone. It is a place for you to center yourself or worship your concept of the Creator. It is a place to put your dreams and wishes so the universe will know what it is you want to manifest. It is a place to create magic.

As with most of the exercises in this book this process is one you must feel rather than think about. It is important to decide if your altar is going to be a permanent structure or a portable one. If you travel a lot or enjoy doing ceremonies out-doors it is useful to have one of each. How you plan on using your altar will influence what materials you choose to place on your altar. It would be difficult to carry around a hundred pound rock or hang a thin cloth to be used as a shelf. Let your-self feel what would be appropriate for you.

Take your time collecting the treasures you will put on your altar. Be open to the process and the objects will show up in your life. What you put on your altar is a matter of choice. My altar seems to collect little treasures like feathers, crystals, coral, and other pretty pieces. Allow your altar to be a dynamic structure rather than a static object in your life. Let it change as you do. Don't hesitate to remove old objects and place new ones on it. After you have gathered all the materials together, you must decide where you want to place the altar.

Once you have everything ready, set aside time to conse-crate your altar. Decide what type of ceremony you will create, how will it look, and if you want to do it alone or with a few trusted friends. Gather everyone and everything together and get ready for the ceremony. I highly recommend using a smudge stick and candles. Smudge sticks are usually available at new age bookstores or you can make your own from dry branches of sage and cedar, or you can choose some of your favorite herbs, whichever seem appropriate. Salt is often placed on altars to symbolize life. Salt can also be used to bless a specific place by sprinkling it around the area.

Fire is a powerful element; I choose to use it in most of my ceremonies. Start by lighting a candle and calling upon the beings of light to assist you. Then light the smudge stick from the candle and allow the smoke to cleanse the area. Allow the smoke to surround each object, all the participants, and the area. Native Americans have used smoke for centuries to remove negative vibrations from an area and to call in the beings of light. Allow the smudge stick to smolder during the ceremony. It will usually go out by itself, but if it doesn't, gently dip it into a glass of water.

Next stand in front of your altar. If it is a fixed altar put it in its designated place; if it is portable, spread it out in front of you. While standing in front of the altar say a simple prayer of consecration. For instance:

> Oh Creator, Great Spirit, Universe, I stand before you, your humble servant. I call upon all the forces of light to energize this holy place. I consecrate this altar to the beings of light. May all that come before it feel the presence of your love, your strength, and your wisdom. May this altar serve to guide me and strengthen my commitment to my sacred self. May I use it always in love and light and may it be an inspiration to me and others. May this be a sacred place for me to bring my dreams and wishes. Bless this place and this dwelling. I give thanks for your presence in my life.

Now begin to place your objects on the altar. Make sure you include several candleholders and if you like incense, an incense holder. Carefully place each item on your altar and when you are finished, spend a few minutes in front of your altar in quiet contemplation. Some people place fresh flowers on their altar every day. Use your altar as you see fit. Some people write letters to the universe about their wishes and dreams. I often place letters about issues I want to release on my altar; after they are there for awhile, I burn them. The ways in which you can use your altar are endless, but always use it in a sacred and loving manner.

Whenever you use a portable altar, make sure you bless it and consecrate it each time you move it. As you continue to use your altar you will feel the energy begin to build in it. Just as churches are made "holy" by the people who have worshipped there, your altar will be made "holy" by your use. I like to meditate in front of my altar. I also put objects on it that I want to energize. As you consecrate your altar you will also create a sacred place.

We create that tool as we do our reality by focusing our attention on it. As we created our altar we made a conscious choice to use the energies that are always around us. We are seldom consciously aware of those energies but we can use them whenever we choose to wake up and focus our attentions on them. There are many energies out there that we can utilize once we become aware of them. The energies of teachers and guides are a wonderful example of that.

SACRED HELPERS

When I first started studying metaphysics I'd hear people talk about their teachers and guides. I had no idea what they were talking about. I now view this concept of teachers as a loving energy—an energy that is noninvasive and willing to help us evolve once we ask for that assistance. I think of them as sacred helpers.

At first, many people perceive this loving energy as a separate entity or person. These sacred helpers are often a part of our soul or spirit that we have in some way forgotten or disowned. They are part of us, but our mind would prefer to see them as separate entities. They only want to help.

I experience the energy of my sacred helpers as a gentle, quiet whisper. It is almost like a gentle breeze beckoning me. When I am centered and still, my next steps or answers become obvious to me. I know the answer will always come if I listen. It may not be in the form I expected, but the answers will always come. At times I get some of my guidance in dreams. At other times it is a feeling, or I'll read or hear something that fits my situation. The guidance is always clear, but I have to be willing to receive it.

When I first began working with these energies, I would sit down to meditate with a pen and pad. I would start out by writing three questions and then go into my meditation. I would relax and make contact with "my teachers," then gently open my eyes and read the first question. The first time I did this, the information I received was so intriguing I didn't bother writing it down. I knew I would remember it, but when I came out of the meditation I had absolutely no memory of what was said. After that, I wrote down the information as I received it. With practice I found that the process of reading and writing did little to disturb my meditation. My intention was to receive guidance from that energy and that is what I experienced.

As you become familiar with these other universes, it is important to train your mind to receive the information. Writing the information down will help your mind acknowledge the validity of the information that you gain in those other universes. As children we often have imaginary playmates, but I'm not convinced that those playmates are imaginary. I believe that as children we can still communicate with beings that exist at different energy levels. As we grow older, we forget how to. We must retrain ourselves so we can again access those levels.

I no longer write out my questions and answers, but I do use my journal to record my experiences during meditations. It's interesting to look back over time and see what my concerns were and what sort of information I was receiving. Now I find it relatively easy to get information on any subject as long as it isn't emotionally charged. When I am emotional about a specific issue, the emotions seem to cloud the connection.

Remembering how to receive information is a process. I find at times that my mind will attempt to fill up the silence. At first it was confusing—I was never sure whether the information was coming from my mind or my sacred helpers. Eventually I could tell where the information came from by the way I felt. When I am in harmony with my higher guidance I sense a gentleness, a sense of connection, a sense of love. When the information is coming from my ego there is a sense of harshness, a sense of trying to convince myself.

Over a period of time we develop our ability of discernment, and begin to know without doubt if the information is valid. If you have to convince yourself of the validity of the information you are receiving, it probably isn't accurate. As I have learned to love and trust myself, I have come to rely more heavily on my inner guidance. Having supportive, loving guidance in my life has been a true gift. The longer I work with that guidance, the more it seems to become a part of me. It comes from within, from my heart.

TEACHER MEDITATION

You can do this meditation alone or in a group. If you do it in a group, have one person guide the group by reading the meditation after everyone has had time to relax. If you are doing it alone, you might want to record the meditation, leaving enough time at the beginning of the tape to relax thoroughly.

In this meditation I've kept the descriptions of the surroundings as vague as possible. That way you can make the experience truly your own rather then a reproduction of mine. Relax and allow whatever you experience to be alright. Release your judgments and expectations so you can enjoy the experience. Some people don't experience a presence immediately; that is fine. Trust that as you continue to repeat the meditation you will connect with your higher guidance.

You begin to walk along a path. It has a sense of familiarity. You feel at peace. You have a sense of excitement. You begin to walk along the path, taking time to observe the surroundings. You take a deep breath of the fresh, clean air. It smells so sweet. You feel free.

Off in the distance you see a structure. You recognize it but you're not sure why. You know you belong there. You feel it beckoning you to come home. You begin moving toward it. As you approach, you feel welcomed, and you're not sure why. You accept that feeling.

You enter the structure. It feels safe, loving, very peaceful. You wonder why it took you so long to come back. You begin to look around. As you do, you sense a loving, kind, and gentle presence. It greets you and you greet it. You open up to the love. You feel extremely loved and protected. There is a gentleness you've longed for. You feel at peace.

(Pause.)

You begin to open up to the presence. You begin to receive impressions and feelings. Not quite words, but almost words. You begin to communicate.

(Long pause. You can ask your question at this point.)

You thank the presence and you know this is just a beginning. You know the presence will be there for you whenever you return. You begin to move about the structure and make it yours. Perhaps a window there and books or a computer there. Arrange it in whatever way you would like. Make it your own. Make it exactly the way you want it.

(Long pause.)

You look around and it feels right. You know you can change it whenever you'd like. In the corner there is a fountain filled with sparkling light. You climb in it and allow the light to cleanse and energize you. It removes the doubt, sadness, and anger. The light fills you with love and laughter. You feel so alive.

(Long pause.)

You dance out of the fountain. You thank the presence. You feel the love. You hesitate for a moment. You'd like to stay forever but you know you will return. Perhaps in your dreams, perhaps in your next meditation. You bid the presence farewell.

As you leave the structure, you notice the path has changed. Everything looks more alive, more beautiful. You feel wonderful. You slowly walk back down the path. You feel much freer and happier than before. You feel connected and loved. Bring that feeling with you.

I suggest you do this meditation several times in order to connect more completely with that presence. After the connection has become comfortable, you can begin the process of writing questions down and asking for the answers. Eventually accessing information from the ethereal level becomes so natural you will no longer need to write down your questions and answers.

Interacting with these energies and working with your altar help you to refocus your mind. It is easy to get so involved in the drama of our life that we forget life is sacred. To make life sacred we simply have to remain conscious.

When I am listening to my mind, I am asleep. I have forgotten who I am and what life is really about. When I listen to my mind I feel alone and isolated; I no longer feel part of the universe. I am caught up in my insignificant plans and my need to control my life in order to feel safe. I have forgotten that I am one with the Creator. I have forgotten that I am merely a humble creation and that I was created in the likeness of that Creator, which means I am a powerful being of light. Those two ideas seem mutually exclusive to my mind—how can I be humble and powerful at the same time?

My sacred self understands that idea fully. And life is joyous when I live it from that perspective.

EXERCISES

1. Writing letters can be an excellent way to focus your attention. I often write letters to the universe. I talk to that creative energy as I would a friend. I write about my fears and any emotional turmoil I have. I also write letters to people with whom I am upset. I never mail those letters but I release a lot of emotions by writing them. Try writing a letter each day to the universe—ask for help, let go of your feelings, and connect. Do it for a month and see how you feel.

2. Write letters about your dreams. Write to the universe and tell it what you would like to experience in your life. Close it with a statement such as: "Your will, not mine." Place the letters on your altar and wait for the miracles to happen.

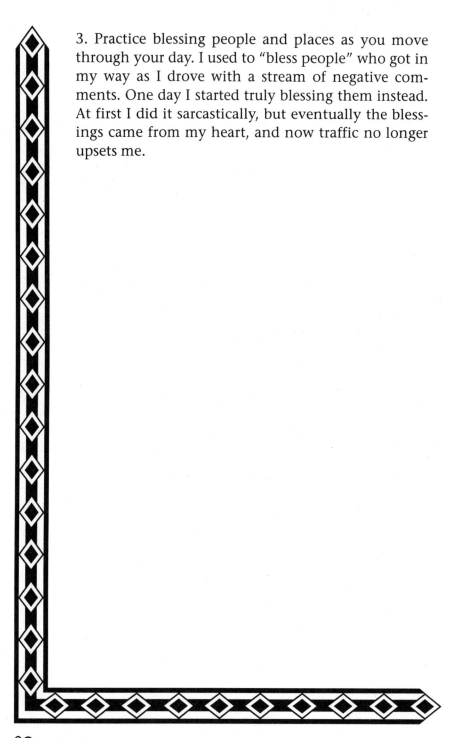

3. Practice blessing people and places as you move through your day. I used to "bless people" who got in my way as I drove with a stream of negative comments. One day I started truly blessing them instead. At first I did it sarcastically, but eventually the blessings came from my heart, and now traffic no longer upsets me.

4. Create a blessing ceremony for your house and then use it to bless your home.

5. Focus your attention on staying awake. Make your life a sacred act.

NOTES

▲▲▲ Chapter Six ▲▲▲

ENERGY

The old woman stood up and motioned for the children to follow her. They had never gone for a walk together before. She held out her hand and twenty small ones quickly reached out to grasp it. Oh, how she loved the little ones, and how they loved her.

It was early spring and the wild flowers were beginning to appear here and there. The world smelled fresh and new. The animals were emerging from the long winter with a host of young ones. The plaintive cry of an eagle soaring overhead could be heard throughout the valley.

The clouds cast wonderful shadows as they danced through the vibrant blue sky. Off in the distance, the river looked like it was filled with diamonds as the sun reflected off its surface.

The old woman found a comfortable place in the shade nearby. The children sat quietly at her feet. "Look at the water and tell me what you see," said the woman.

The children all began speaking at once and she laughed. "One at a time, please."

The littlest girl said, "I see the sun making sparkles on the surface and leaves floating along, and I also see the Great Spirit's face in the waterfall."

"Very good, little one. Which way do the leaves flow?" asked the ancient one.

"That is silly, with the river of course," said one of the children.

"What of the birds? Do they live on the ground and walk on all fours?"

"Of course not, Grandmother. They fly and live in the trees."

"Does the river flow uphill or down?"

"Water always flows down, just as summer follows spring," said one of the boys.

"Yes, little ones, there is a definite order and flow to life," said the old woman. "The Great Spirit has made a world that is predictable. When we take time to observe nature we can know what will happen next. We can tell if it is going to rain or what kind of winter it is going to be by the signs."

"It is important to listen to Mother Earth carefully. She can be a loving teacher or a harsh task master. In our lives we all have many teachers but we must get quiet enough to hear them. There are many spirits that walk this land, some are loving and some are souls who have lost their way. Always remember to call upon your protectors to keep you safe. Listen to your heart and you will be safe. Listen to your head and you will get lost."

"Watch the signs in nature and you will always know which way to turn. By seeing with your heart, you can tell who has been here and who will be here soon. Watch the signs in your life, and you will also know which way to turn."

"We each have an individual path to walk during our time on the earth. The Great Spirit created us with a purpose and definite direction. At times it is hard to find our path because we get so busy living. We stop listening to our hearts, and we begin talking to ourselves. When we listen to ourselves, our troubles really begin. You must always connect with your spirit guides and listen to your heart. Love yourself and all other beings. Walk softly upon the earth, move quietly and listen to the whispers."

"You, little Fawn Eyes, will be a great storyteller. And you, my boy, will be a great warrior, and one of you will be chief and the greatest spiritual teacher to walk the path in many years."

"Which one, Grandmother?" asked one of the older boys. They all began to look at one another with awe and caution.

"Search your heart and you will know. Close your eyes and breathe deeply. Feel the energies around you. Quiet your mind and focus on your heart. Ask yourself which way you must go, where your path will lead you, how you can best serve the Great Spirit. Let the energy build around you and let yourself know truth. Listen to the river as it effortlessly flows to the ocean. What do you hear? What does nature have to tell you? Breathe deeply, my little ones, and rest in the loving embrace of the great Earth Mother."

The sun felt so warm and comforting that the old woman soon fell fast asleep. She dreamed about the past, while the children dreamed about their futures.

As you learn to follow your heart, life becomes much easier. We each have chosen to come here for a specific purpose. If in your heart you have chosen to be a teacher, you won't find your happiness until you become a teacher. There is a time to reap and a time to sow—the difficult part is knowing what time it is and what your role is. Once you know how to listen and to follow the energy, the process becomes easier.

Energy is defined in the dictionary as available power. Most of this path is a process of learning to become sensitive to the energies that are always around us. Most of the time we are unaware of all the other realities that simultaneously coexist with our universe. As we become sensitive to the various energies we can begin to harness and use them.

Everything is made up of energy. The page you are reading is actually a mass of electrons swirling around a nucleus of protons and neutrons. Those elements can be broken down further and further until the particles are so small that they react in ways that don't make sense to our rational linear minds. The elements are affected by the beliefs of the observer: if the observer expects them to act as waves, they do; and if the observer thinks they are particles, they act like particles. They seem to have consciousness.

Our universe and our lives are an illusion. This page seems solid yet it is really mostly empty space. The chair that your body is sitting on also seems solid, but it isn't. Nor is your body. Everything in this universe is actually made up of predominately empty space. Everything is composed of atoms and the electrons swirl so quickly that objects appear solid.

Whenever you watch a movie, you think you are seeing the objects and actors move. What you are actually seeing is a series of still pictures which appear to move when they are rapidly projected one after another. The illusion is that they are moving, just as it is an illusion that everything in this universe is solid.

Life is like the movies in the sense that it is an illusion that seems real. Life begins to make more sense when viewed strictly as energy. The only thing that is real in this world is love, but it certainly doesn't look that way. All you have to do is watch the news, and you could argue that this world is an unsafe place. It appears that this reality is filled with lack and limitations and that you have to protect yourself.

As we learn to view this world from an energy level, the operating rules of the universe seem to change. Everything in this universe is composed totally of energy. I believe that this energy has consciousness. For lack of a better word, I call that consciousness love. It is really a combination of a sense of love, safety, peace, unconditional acceptance, and contentment.

Collectively that energy is what people usually describe as God. Whatever you happen to call that energy, it does have consciousness, and when you align yourself with it, your life becomes wonderful. You realize that you are safe, completely safe. After all, you too are made up of that energy.

Once you step out of the illusion, you can remember at a core level that you are safe. You can live without fear and can experience love constantly. You can begin to live from your sacred center and become your sacred self. Your ego knows fear; your sacred self knows only peace. Whoever or whatever created this universe created it so that it is completely child proof, safe for you to explore. There are no sharp edges, you can never truly be hurt. At an energy level you are eternal, immortal, and infinite. There is no margin for error. You can never cease to exist; you are safe.

FEELING SAFE

How would your life be different if you absolutely knew to the very core of your being that you were constantly safe? If you absolutely knew you were safe and that you existed in a universe that was composed totally of love, how would that change the way you lead your life? Take a few moments to think about it. Think of all the decisions you have made in your life based on fear. Think of all the pain you have felt in your life because of your mind's need to be right in order to feel safe. When there is no need to be right, there is no need for judgment or prejudice. People and nations would not need to control one another, and war would become obsolete.

Take a few minutes right now to imagine a world built on the premise that everyone is safe and perfect just as they are. Relax and imagine what that would feel like. Notice your mind's resistance to the idea (remember, it always wants to be right). Set any resistance aside and relax into the feeling of safety. Repeat to yourself that you are safe. Close your eyes and breathe deeply. Imagine yourself breathing in that feeling of safety and allow yourself to relax into it.

Take a few minutes to sit with the sensation of being safe. Allow the feeling to expand and grow. Let yourself feel completely safe. You are invincible because there is nothing that can really hurt you.

Now allow yourself to be surrounded by love. Pretend you are floating on a bed that is composed of pure love. Keep repeating to yourself that you are loved, you are love, and all there is is love. Let your heart open and feel truly loved. Imagine the whole world loving you. What would that be like?

Now take time to write about how that feels. Expand on the feelings, make up a story. Do whatever is necessary to allow yourself to feel safe and loved. This is an exercise in becoming sensitive to the energy that is around us. You can tap into love at any time. Safety or fear: the choice is always yours to make.

You swim in a sea of energy, and you can use or define it in any way you choose. Unfortunately, most of the time you allow your mind to choose for you. Your mind, or ego, only knows fear. Whenever you listen to it, you generally believe whatever it tells you about what is going on. It is a merchant of doom. When you make the choice to listen to your mind you are guaranteed to have feelings of discomfort, lack, and limitations. When you listen to your heart, or your sacred self, you are guaranteed feelings of love, safety, and serenity.

As you step back into the realm of energy, your choices once again expand and become limitless. The book *A Course in Miracles* talks about seeing life differently. As you become more sensitive to the energy levels around you, you automatically begin to "see" differently. You begin to experience the truth instead of living in the illusion created by your mind.

FEELING THE ENERGY

You must first become more aware of all the energies that surround you. Your mind filters out the majority of information that is constantly impacting you; if it didn't, you would be overwhelmed. As you read this book, if you begin to think about the housework you should be doing or what's for dinner, it becomes difficult to concentrate. The same is true when you are having a conversation with a friend or associate. If you were unable to filter out the background noises and distractions, it would be confusing and difficult to carry on a conversation.

For a moment, close your eyes and describe the room you are sitting in. What colors are in your room? How many of the details are you aware of? Open your eyes and notice everything blue in the room. Now, close your eyes and remember everything red. Are you beginning to see how your mind operates? Observe it for a few days. It is an interesting revelation to realize how colored your perspective of reality really is.

As you begin to increase your awareness of the energies that surround you, all you are actually doing is turning up the volume on something that already exists. When I began doing these exercises, I made them much more difficult than was necessary. I was quite dramatic about the process and kept thinking that I was developing extrasensory perception. I became intense; I acted like I believed that I was creating these universes rather than just sensing them. All I was doing was focusing my attention so I could turn up the volume. I was focusing on one level and tuning out another.

An easy place to begin is with your own life force, or energy. For a moment hold your hands about six inches apart and focus your attention on the area between your hands. Slowly move your hands in and out and concentrate in a relaxed manner on the area between your hands. Focus your attention on the surface of your hands. After a few minutes they will begin to feel slightly sticky. The area between them will seem to take on a life of its own. You will begin to notice a change in the way your hands feel as you move them. Move them apart suddenly and then quickly together. How does that feel?

As you quiet your mind, you will begin to feel your own energy field. Once you are aware of how it feels, begin to move your hands over your body without touching yourself and notice how that feels. Do you feel any changes in temperature as you move over the various parts of your body? Do some places feel tighter than others? Relax and without judgment notice how your energy field feels.

On an energy level, a human being looks like a large, luminous egg. This energy field, or aura, extends about five feet beyond a being's center. If you are in a group, have two people stand about fifteen feet apart facing each other. With their eyes closed have them slowly begin moving toward one another and stop when they can feel the other person's energy. Most people will stop a few feet away. The first time I did this exercise my partner was Sister Sarita, and I stopped about five feet away from her. I could feel her energy moving toward me like a gentle wind that was swirling around the room.

We are always aware of other people's energy, yet we've learned to ignore it. We don't consciously think about it. Have you ever met someone and disliked them on sight? Have you ever walked into a room where two people had just been arguing? On the occasions I have, I've felt uncomfortable. I used to think it was I who was doing something wrong, now I know I am merely picking up old energy that I can simply leave behind. We already have these abilities. They are part of our instinctual nature; we must merely give ourselves permission to remember how to use them.

Locations also have their own inherent energy field regardless of what has been going on within it. Have you ever walked into a room and immediately felt comfortable? On the surface there was no apparent reason for those feelings, but you felt good anyway. Practice going into different places and sensing the energy. Practice with various locations until you are comfortable picking up the background energy. Does a church feel different from a bar or a supermarket?

Next, practice with objects. Sit in a chair and see what you feel. We all leave an energy imprint or after-image on anything we contact. See if you can become aware of what has been left behind.

When I was developing my sensitivities to the various energies, I would go to a public place, a mall or anywhere numbers of people pass through. I would find a bench or a wall, sit down, close my eyes, and go into a light meditative state. With my eyes closed, I would observe the energy fields of people as they approached.

At first I would sit and merely try to tell when someone was approaching. When I was able to do that, I then began to observe their energy. I would try to get a feel for them energetically, and then open my eyes and observe them objectively. I found that children and adults felt different, as did men and women. Men felt more angular while women felt softer. To me children felt like bubbles of light and adults felt much heavier. Teenagers were very unusual energetically, especially if they were on a date.

Miguel suggested that I observe people, suspending any judgment. I found it difficult to observe people without immediately forming a judgment about them. My mind always wanted to attach a story to what it saw. As you practice sensing people, you eventually begin to get hunches about their personalities and lives. Try to remain impartial as you receive this information.

Interpreting what we sense is a matter of our perspective. As a child, I loved lying on my back to watch clouds. I would spend hours finding creatures and animal forms in them. I often wondered what it would feel like to touch one. I got a chart that showed pictures of the various types of clouds and memorized their names. I knew that I wanted to play on them forever, bouncing and falling into their softness. I really thought that they were solid, yet fluffy and soft.

One day my dad took me flying in his Piper Cub. He left the cockpit open as we rose into the air. I knew we would eventually fly through a cloud and I would get to touch it. I was overjoyed by the idea. When we flew into the first cloud, I reached my little arm out with a great deal of excitement. When I touched the cloud, I was devastated to find there was nothing there; it was an illusion. All my hand felt was slightly damp and a little cooler.

Over the years, I have interpreted that incident in many ways. I have used it as an example of the folly of expectations, of the world as an illusion, and a variety of other examples. I have never lost my fascination with clouds, and I enjoy watching them interact with the mountains in Hawaii. The other day I was driving to work and watching the clouds gently caress the mountaintops. As I drove along the coast, I was struck by the idea that the clouds were touching the mountains in the same way the Creator or Great Spirit touches our lives. Their touch is gentle, almost illusive, yet their presence is beautiful and healing. None of these interpretations are right or wrong; they are a matter of my perspective. As you observe people's energies, you might want to think about clouds.

TURNING UP OUR PHYSICAL SENSES

This is a fun exercise that will help you increase your awareness of yourself and your environment. Get comfortable in a place where you won't be disturbed for fifteen or twenty minutes. Relax and concentrate on your breathing. Allow yourself to go into a light meditative state.

After you are totally relaxed, gently open your eyes a bit and with a soft gaze say to yourself "I see." Then mentally list all the things you can see, paying attention to the details. Close your eyes, relax, and mentally say to yourself "I feel," and mentally list all the sensations you are noticing. Notice where and how your body is contacting the surface you are resting on. Notice your clothing, how your hair touches your body, and how the air moves around you.

Next, continue this process with your hearing. As you relax, say to yourself "I hear." Now notice all the sounds you can hear. Focus your attention on your hearing and notice all the noises in your world. Continue the process by focusing on your sense of smell and then on your sense of taste. Really take time to explore each of your senses. Before ending this meditation, repeat the entire process at least four more times.

The first time I did this meditation was just before I went to bed. The next morning I got up and took my dog for a walk, as I usually did. I was absolutely amazed. The first thing I noticed were the sounds and smells of someone cutting grass about three blocks away. Then I began to notice the colors. They were much more vivid and alive. I felt like a little gremlin had slipped into my head overnight and turned up the volume on all my senses—it was wonderful. The effect only lasted a few hours, but I knew how it felt to be fully conscious of my world.

These days I usually get up around sunrise, sit at my desk, and write in my journal. One morning, my mind was grumbling about being up so early, but as I was writing in my journal, I heard a mourning dove coo and my mood shifted. I had never noticed one singing outside my window at that hour before, now I hear them every morning.

Depending upon your perspective, one of the gifts or curses of being a human being is that once we know something, we can't *not* know it. Our minds love to be right and they love to delete unpleasant facts from our reality. They prefer their version of reality to the truth. Our focus is frequently limited. This exercise helps us go beyond those limits.

INORGANIC BEINGS

Inorganic beings are entities that exist on the ethereal level. These beings live on emotions just as we need food, air, and water to survive. They literally feed on emotions generated by other beings, especially humans and animals. Some feed on emotions like fear, anger, and sadness while others feed on joy. Angels, fairies, and gnomes are inorganic beings that feed on joy and laughter. Angels get their sustenance by helping people and by creating joy in their lives.

There are a variety of universes out there. Some of them are filled with anger and hostility. Beings from those universes can be rather troublesome. At times when I was studying with Miguel, I would suddenly feel depressed or angry for no apparent reason. Eventually, I realized that an inorganic being had attached itself to me. The first time this happened I was terrified. I went to class that night furious. I wanted to leave class but I knew that leaving would be a big mistake. As we went into our meditation Miguel sat opposite me. I fought every one of his suggestions to relax. He patiently worked with me energetically until the being left. I was so relieved that I began to cry.

After the meditation, I asked Miguel what had happened. He laughed and described how the being had tried to scare him.

I knew it scared me. For a long time after that it seemed like a weekly occurrence, and I spent a lot of time running to Miguel to be saved from these beings. When I got tired of feeling like a victim of these entities, I got angry and told them to leave me alone. Much to my surprise, they did.

These beings cannot hurt us in any way unless we let them. We have total dominion on this plane, so if we tell them to leave and mean it, they must leave. If we passively give them our permission to exist by showing them fear, we give them the power to terrorize us. These inorganic beings are a gift, they teach us to go beyond our fear and they force us to step back into our sacred centers. When we are in that center nothing can hurt us. Learning how to deal with these entities teaches us about self-empowerment.

Occasionally some of these beings are very powerful and require a little extra effort to remove. The easiest way to do so is by having a ceremony. This allows us to focus our attention and step into our sacred centers.

RELEASING NEGATIVE BEINGS

You can make this ceremony as simple or as elaborate as you like. To perform this ceremony you will need a smudge stick, a candle, and lavender or some other pleasant scent. Start by calling on your protector. Once you feel its presence, say a simple prayer of protection, such as:

Creator, Great Spirit, Universal Energy, I call upon your love and your protection. I call upon the beings of light and all those beings that help lost souls. See this being that has lost its way home. It believes it is of the dark; it has forgotten it is of the light. Please surround it with your love and gently guide it back to the light so that it may heal. Please surround this place and all within it with your love and protection. I give thanks.

Light the candle and smudge stick. Thoroughly smudge the area and yourself and allow the smoke to clear the area of any negativity. Then stand in the center of the room and declare that only beings of light are allowed in your aura or dwelling place. Call upon beings of light to protect you and your location. Demand that all lower energy forces leave now and return to the light. Declare that this place is only for those who live in love and light. See yourself and the room filled with and surrounded by a bright white light. Know you are safe and protected. Sprinkle the lavender oil around the room.

Make sure you protect yourself for a few days after you release one of these beings. One way to do this is to visualize your energy field and see it filled with white light. Mentally seal it with white light and see flecks of green and pink light floating around your body. Do this several times a day for the next few days. You tend to be more open to negative beings once one has been removed, and this process will help seal up your energy field. If you again feel a negative presence, repeat the ceremony.

The easiest thing to do is make sure you don't attract one in the first place. If you remember to call upon your protector and keep yourself surrounded by white light, they can't get near you. I always bless any place I work or live. I cleanse and fill it with beings of light specifically called upon to protect the place and anyone who enters.

EXERCISES

1. Practice putting on the energy of _____. If you want to have more money, practice putting on the energy of abundance. Visualize yourself in a cloak that is filled with the energy of abundance, or whatever else you want to experience in your life. If you want to be more gregarious, imagine putting on a cloak that makes your friendlier. Practice putting on various forms of positive energy.

2. Practice feeling the emotional energy fields around you. Notice all the details and all the sensations that your mind would normally filter out about the events around you.

3. List all the decisions you have made based on fear and notice the results. Then choose to feel safe for an entire day and notice how you feel. Practice living in your sacred center.

NOTES

▲▲▲ CHAPTER SEVEN ▲▲▲

SHADOWS

Many thousands of years ago men and women walked the earth as equals. They shared their lives and the earth with reverence, and walked with dignity. Neither was superior nor inferior—they were equal in all things. The Earth Mother provided for them abundantly, and they lived in harmony with the earth and all the creatures.

They honored the Mother and Father God as well as the spirit that resides in everything. It was a time of great balance and harmony. There was no fear or worry, only peace and love.

Then a famine came upon the land. Since many of the women were nursing or with child, it seemed logical for the men to become the providers. It was easier for them to travel so they went off in search of food. Time went on and the famine continued. The weather was changing and the winters were getting longer. It snowed almost all year so the humans were forced to move south in search of warmth and food.

The famine, and thus the process of hunting and moving, went on for many generations. Eventually, men and women were no longer physical equals because of the division of strenuous activity. Men had become stronger and women had slowly come to be considered the physically weaker sex.

Eventually the famine ended, but equality had been forgotten. Women had given up their power for the illusion of being cared for, while men had given up their femininity, or intuitive nature, to be in control. As time went on, women remained more in tune with their spirituality and men became stronger physically. Men suppressed their feminine nature and women suppressed their masculine nature. In a sense, women gave up their power and men gave up their souls.

A time of darkness fell upon the earth. People no longer lived in harmony with nature, they lived in large communities the land could not support. The waters and the air became dirty and many animals no longer existed.

Some women continued to honor the earth spirits. They continued to perform sacred ceremonies and use their powers for healing. The male priests were threatened by their power so they called them evil and said that they came from the darkness. Millions of women were burned as witches because of their powers; they were able to heal and still had a personal relationship with their sacred selves. Although some of them continued to honor the Goddess, which was threatening to the status of male superiority, women were no longer honored in society. Nurturing and softness were thought to be signs of weakness. Humans became shadows of their former selves. Eventually most women also gave up their spiritual connection. The darkness was almost complete.

Both men and women suffered; they felt lost and unfulfilled. People no longer understood their sacred natures. They had forgotten that they were not their bodies and that their lives were a gift bestowed upon them by the Creator. They had lost their way home. They no longer communicated directly with their Creator; they looked to others to tell them how to worship God.

Both men and women began to feel empty and disconnected. Slowly people began to ask questions and search for answers. They began to reconnect with their spirituality. Slowly they began to reconnect with their sacred natures. It started first with women as they began to reclaim their personal power. Then they reclaimed their spirituality.

That part of each of them that had become a distant shadow, their spirituality, slowly came into focus. Women began to honor their power and men began to accept the softness of women. In groups and by themselves they began to search for their sacred natures. They began to honor themselves and each other.

Love again became the language of the land. Instead of anger and competition, people began to cooperate. Peace and harmony followed once they rediscovered the goddess within.

For many centuries we have been disconnected from our spiritual centers. Until recently, a person's feminine nature was not held in high regard. Intuition and connecting with spirit was punishable by death not too long ago. We generally put our attention on things we value, and often our spirituality doesn't seem valuable.

Both men and women have a feminine side. In it resides our connection with our spirituality, our intuition and our receptive nature. It is the part of us most closely aligned with our sacred self. We can only connect with our spirituality from our feminine side.

We are spiritual beings who are having a physical experience; we are not physical beings having a spiritual experience. We are spirit, and we must learn to honor our true natures. It is the only way we will be free of fear.

Crows' fascination with shiny objects often allows them to overcome their fear of human beings. They override their fear so they can steal the objects for their nests. As human beings, we are a lot like crows: we love bright things. Habitually, most people tend to focus their attention on the bright things in life. Our eyes naturally focus on the light areas of objects rather than the darker spaces. Glance around the room for a moment and notice where your eyes come to rest. What do you notice first? Chances are you focused on the bright spots. We do the same thing with our emotions.

Emotionally, most people prefer to be happy and avoid crying and to be joyous rather than angry. For a long time after I began pursuing my spiritual path, I felt like a failure if I was less than completely mellow and joyously happy. When I wasn't content, I knew that I must be doing something wrong. I felt like a failure if I felt anger. At the time I didn't realize that emotions were part of being human. There are no good or bad emotions, there are simply feelings.

In truth, without the darkness we would be unable to see. It is the contrast in life that defines the objects in our reality. If everything was white we would be unable to see, everything would look the same. Without sadness we would not understand or know what joy is—there would be nothing with which to compare it.

When Miguel and I first began working with shadows, I became aware of how much fear they evoked within me, and I wasn't even sure why. At some level, I felt there were horrible monsters lurking in the shadows. As a child I was certain there were monsters living under my bed. I felt they would come out and get me as soon as my mother turned out the lights. As an adult I still carried that fear on an unconscious level.

When you look at our mythology, the dark side is always painted as evil and sinister. Have you ever wondered why?

At an instinctual level, we all fear the dark, and our mythology merely reflects that fear. When we were living in caves, the dark was not safe; saber-toothed tigers and other animals of prey lurked in the shadows. Emotionally, we also fear the shadowy parts of our personality.

I knew that if I looked deep inside myself I would find a dark, evil being that was unlovable. I grew up in a dysfunctional family and I had learned to be ashamed of myself. I was certain there was something wrong with me. When I would get angry, it felt like there was an uncontrollable monster inside me. I feared my darker emotions and personality. I feared the shadows within myself.

Shadows

As I began exploring shadows, I did find beings lurking in them, but I found that they were not necessarily threatening. One of the reasons our mythology includes those fears of monsters in the shadows and darkness is that shadows are a door to other realms, universes that are unfamiliar. Our minds often define the unknown as threatening. People also intuitively feel the presence of these beings, the ones that exist in those other realities. Since they are part of the unknown, we fear them.

While walking on the beach one day, I met a being that was dressed in a long black cape. As soon as I saw him my heart began pounding. I was certain he was evil because he was dressed in black. Talk about stereotyping!

After a few moments, I noticed that my surroundings had changed. I was alone on the beach with him, and the sky had become a strange color. I realized that somehow I had managed to enter another reality. I was terrified, and I immediately tried running away from him. When I looked back he was gone and the beach was again filled with people.

A few days later, I mentioned him to one of the other advanced apprentices. I was pleased with myself because I had managed to get away from him. She looked at me and smiled. She told me not to assume that all beings dressed in black were evil. She suggested that I might have lost an opportunity to learn something more valuable than how to get away.

A few days later, I again saw this entity as I was walking along the beach. This time I swallowed my fears and asked him what he wanted. He smiled and wrapped his cloak around me and then disappeared. I felt a little unsettled but didn't think too much about it. The next day when I went to work, everyone ignored me. I felt like I was invisible. After a while, I felt annoyed, and then I remembered the stranger in the cape.

That afternoon right after work I went to the beach to look for him. As soon as I relaxed and started walking, I saw him. I asked him what was happening, and he told me that he had come to teach me about invisibility. I told him that I was not amused. He laughed and began working with me. The lessons he taught me were not very pleasant at times, but they were

▲▲▲ 117

beneficial. I learned to appreciate the shadows more. I tried not to judge things before I was sure of their meaning.

Shadows contain a wonderful world of unlimited possibilities. There is an old story that the gods were sitting around one day talking. They had decided to give humans the gift of their godhood, but they weren't sure where to put it. They did not want to put it anywhere too obvious; they did not want the humans to find it easily. The gods wanted to make sure that they wouldn't find this power until they knew how to use it wisely. They argued endlessly, trying to decide where to put it. Finally they decided to put it where no one would ever think of looking. They put the gift deep inside of each of the humans— in their shadows.

As with everything else in life, exploring the shadows starts with intention and with a change in focus. It is a matter of noticing the shadows. Once you begin to look at them you can begin to "see" what is in them. Until Miguel told me to focus my attention on the shadows, I doubt if I ever consciously noticed them except as a contrast to the light. Once I began observing them and got beyond my fear of the unknown I was amazed at the way I began to feel. I usually felt a sense of peace and oneness when I was able to relax and focus on the shadows. Sometimes I was afraid, but soon I only felt the love.

FOCUSING ON THE SHADOWS

Water is a wonderful place to begin working with shadows. One of the easiest places to start focusing on the shadows is in a lake or ocean. It is best to wait until the sun is low in the horizon, and it is over the water in front of you. When the sun is right, sensing other universes is easier.

Begin by focusing on the ripples on the water's surface. Notice the contrast between the lighter and darker areas of the water. At first the lighter areas will draw your attention, but continue to focus on the darker areas. The lighter areas may

Shadows

seem more alive while the shadows feel dead. You are simply unfamiliar with the energies in the shadows.

Continue focusing on the shadows, the darker areas. Call upon your protector and relax. As you continue to gaze at the shadows you will begin to feel something pulling at you. It will feel as if you are trying to remember something, like there is something right on the edge of your reality calling to you. Let it call to you; allow yourself to open up and sense its presence.

If you begin to feel fear rising within you, allow it to pass through you and dissipate. Remind yourself that you are not the fear. Try to experience the fear as an energy floating around you. Rather than thinking you are afraid, say to yourself that there is an energy of fear present. You are not the fear; you are an energy that is untouchable by the fear. Remember that the fear isn't real, it is an illusion. The only thing that is real is love; everything else—especially your fear—is an illusion.

Continue to relax and focus your attention on the shadows until you feel a doorway slowly opening. Keeping your protector close beside you, permit your consciousness to begin slowly drifting into that doorway. You will step into a universe filled with beings that are fluid and light. Each person will experience these beings differently. I perceive them as loving and healing energy. For lack of a better name I think of them as water beings, beings unique to a particular body of water that have different energies and personalities.

Give yourself time to sense them. Try not to label what you are feeling. Trust the process. For as long as you have patience, relax and remain open; eventually you will be able to sense their universe. Openmindedness is very important, as is being gentle with yourself. Allow your process to be your process, and let it unfold as it will. Do not judge your experience.

The first time I did this exercise Miguel told me to climb a tree that was located in his favorite beach park. I felt extremely foolish as I struggled to climb up the tree. Next he told me to stare at the water, and all I was able to perceive or sense for a long time was the ripples on the surface of the water. I felt inadequate and certain that I would never be able to do this task correctly. He wouldn't tell me what I was looking for, so I became frustrated. When I suddenly felt something pulling at me, I thought I was losing my mind. The next thing I knew, I saw Miguel walking away from the tree and I had to scramble down to catch up with him.

Eventually I learned how to enter those universes, but at first I was so hard on myself that it was a much more arduous task than was necessary. My incessant need to judge and compare my experience to others' made it much harder. Be gentle and loving with yourself; it will be much easier if you let go and trust your process. Eventually you will go beyond your mind's limited perspective, but not as long as you are holding onto your judgments of yourself and your process.

After you have become familiar with the shadows in the water, you can begin to explore them in other areas as well. I have always enjoyed creatures that live in trees. Find a large shade tree somewhere and focus on the shadows. Look at the center of the tree, and focus on the shadows contained within the leaves. Call upon your protector, relax, and breathe deeply. Notice the shadows and allow your consciousness to begin to shift. After a few minutes, your consciousness will begin to shift, and you will become aware of the entities in the tree. In my experience trees are not a doorway as much as they are a residence for ethereal beings. I have found the beings that "live" there to be gentle and loving.

Visit a variety of trees in different areas and see how they feel. Notice how pine trees feel compared to flower or broadleaf trees. Over time see how the feeling of the trees changes with the seasons. Practice being more sensitive to the various energies that reside in our reality.

All shadows contain doorways to the ethereal. The night is also a time when the separation between our reality and the other universes becomes thinner. That is one of the reasons primitive peoples created so many myths about the night. Since they were more aware of the energies around them, they sensed the ethereal worlds. People tend to fear what they don't understand, so we create myths to explain what we are sensing. Sunrise and sunset are times of day when inorganic beings tend to be much more active.

SHADOWS IN THE SOUNDS

Miguel often talked about shadows. He stressed how important the shadows were, how they give our world an added dimension. One day he stole another apprentice's shadow and scared him silly. After we had worked with shadows for a while, he told me to listen for the shadows in sounds. For a long time, I wasn't sure what he meant.

One day I was taking my dog for a walk before dawn. It was a beautiful day and the world was beginning to awaken. As I passed a yucca tree, a bird began to sound her morning song. In that instant I heard the shadows in her song. I stood transfixed by the beauty of the sound or lack of it. I realized that the shadows were the spaces between the sounds, and they were glorious. All that day I listened to the silences between the noises and a whole new world opened up to me.

Try it for a day. Go out in nature and listen to the spaces, listen to the silences. As you focus your attention on the spaces, you will be amazed at the beauty. Words can't even come close to explaining what a wonderful experience it is. Whenever I get caught up in my head, all I have to do is listen to the silences and my whole perspective changes. The world looks much different and more peaceful.

See what your mind tries to do with the silences. Step into the silence and see how it feels. Where does it take you? Relax and enjoy the silence. It is a gift few people ever experience.

FACING OUR SHADOWS

Remember the story of Peter Pan? He was upset when he lost his shadow. Without our shadows, we would no longer be three dimensional. Whether it is our physical shadow or our emotional shadow, both give us depth. Our emotional shadow contains all those behaviors and emotions we would prefer to keep hidden from everyone, including ourselves. The only way to free ourselves is to face all of our emotional baggage and release it. Denial eventually stops working and we must face ourselves head on. When we do look at our shadowy sides, we find that they contain many useful behaviors once they are redirected.

As we face our shadows we begin to realize that our complete selves are acceptable—the so-called good, bad, and indifferent parts are all lovable. As we release the judgments we have about ourselves, we can achieve a greater sense of personal freedom.

In the following meditation, perhaps for the first time, you will acknowledge your whole self. You begin to see the truth about all the parts you have hidden from yourself and from the world for years. Only then can you begin to love yourself unconditionally.

MEDITATION

Find yourself standing in a field. It is a beautiful field. The air smells fresh and clean. There are fluffy white clouds overhead. The sky is the most beautiful blue you have ever seen. You notice a path leading into the woods. You feel a sense of excitement and anticipation as you begin to walk along the path. You are peaceful and relaxed. The path feels soft underfoot. The air smells sweet. You notice the sun filtering through the leaves. The light is magical. The path slowly winds its way through the forest. There is a wonderful sense of peace. The birds call gently.

(Long pause.)

Slowly, you see a clearing off in the distance. It seems to be flooded in a beautiful white light. There is a gentle mist swirling in the clearing. It is very inviting. You feel a sense of reverence, a sense of love, an atmosphere of peace and forgiveness. You enter the clearing. In the center is a magnificent altar. It is luminous and inviting. You gently and quietly approach it.

Shadows

The mist swirls lovingly around your ankles. The far side of the altar is totally surrounded with mist. As you stand in front of the altar, you are filled with love for yourself, the world, and everything in it. The feeling is so powerful your heart feels incredibly full. You kneel down and give thanks.

(Long pause.)

Slowly out of the mists your shadow emerges. At first you are angry and disgusted. You are afraid to face it. As it emerges you notice its eyes; you see the sadness there. The love wells up in your being. You look steadily at it. You let your emotions flow freely. You see your shadow as a wounded being in need of your love and forgiveness.

(Long pause.)

You ask its forgiveness. You forgive yourself. You forgive your shadow. The love surrounds you.

(Long pause.)

Your shadow steps around the altar toward you. You notice how frail it is. You gently pick it up and place it on the altar. The light surrounds it. The shadow begins to glow. It begins to smile, and a look of peace comes over it. Slowly the sadness drains out of its eyes. You feel the love and peace in your heart as well. The shadow sits up and looks at you with love. You embrace. You feel whole at last. You allow your energies to become one. You are joyous and light. Allow the healing to take place.

(Long pause.)

You feel completely free. You kneel at the altar. You give thanks. You forgive yourself for any wrongs you feel you have done. It is such a freeing experience. You forgive and you are forgiven.

(Long pause.)

You get up and slowly leave the clearing, knowing you can return whenever you choose. You feel wonderful, much freer and happier than before. Bring that feeling with you.

This is a healing meditation. Repeat it as often as you wish. Feel the energy of your perfect nature and let go of the past. Allow your shadow to begin talking to you.

One way to get to know your shadow is by observing it firsthand. After you are familiar with working with shadows, go for a walk on a beach or a place where there is a great deal of sand. The best time to do this is when the sun is low in the sky so your shadow is long. As you walk along the beach, focus on your shadow and begin by observing it, just as you did with the water and the trees.

Spend time with your shadow. It is uncanny how it will change and feel like a separate entity. Talk to it, get to know it and yourself in the process. Relax and have fun with this part of you. Remember how upset Peter Pan was when he lost his shadow. Make friends with yours.

EXERCISES

1. Write about your shadowy emotions, your secrets. How does your need to keep them secret cause pain and turmoil in your life?

2. Spend time outside at sunrise and sunset. These are times of energy transition; the door to the ethereal opens and closes. Notice what you sense and observe. Can you feel the doorway opening?

3. Go for a walk on the beach when the sun is low in the horizon and observe your shadow. How does it feel? Try communicating with it. Watch other people's shadows as well—what can you learn from them?

CHAPTER EIGHT

MIRROR MEDITATIONS

Long ago, deep in the forest there was a place filled with magic. The ancient ones used to gather there when the moon was full and teach any who were brave enough to come to them. The moonlight filtered gracefully through the leaves, creating wonderful shadows and shafts of light that seemed to come from heaven. As the moon reflected off the surface of the stream, rainbows could be seen on the neighboring rocks. The surface of the stream looked like a field of diamonds. This place was eternally spring.

The sounds of the stream blended hypnotically with the songs of the birds and whispering of the wind. It was a magical place indeed, a place of perfect peace. The air was heavy with the smell of moss and damp leaves—earthy and sweet.

One day, a young girl was walking through the forest. She was curious about the noises from the stream; they seemed to call her name. She knelt by the edge of the stream and was transfixed by the reflection she saw. It seemed to dance and swirl and the diamonds in the water broke it up into hundreds of other shapes. A flower floated by and began to swirl in a tiny whirlpool. She found herself lost in thought.

Her eyes followed the flower as it swirled slowly in front of her. Round and round it went; she couldn't bring herself to look away. Suddenly she felt herself pulled downward, down and down into a swirling tunnel. She felt herself plummeting headlong into a darkened sky filled with stars.

At first she was terrified, but after a time she realized she was no longer falling. She was actually flying, and she felt free. She would hurl herself at a star cluster filled with rainbows only to veer off at the last moment. For what seemed like an eternity she played and danced through the universe. The stars were magical and she quietly thought to herself that she could fly forever. But after a time she noticed that she was lonely.

As she flew along she softly wished she had someone to talk to. At that very instant she found herself seated opposite a gentle and wise old woman. As she looked into her eyes she saw all the stars reflected there, and she felt an incredible surge of love run through her entire body.

"Who are you?" asked the little girl.

"I have many names, my daughter. Choose the one which most pleases you. I have been called simply the Goddess by some, and others have called me the Earth Mother. I have too many names to remember them all," said the old woman.

"I have always loved the earth and I have heard tales about Earth Mother. She is loving, wise, and gentle, and she loves the animals. I think I will call you that. But who are you, and why am I here? How did I get here?" asked the girl.

"One question at a time, little one. You are in a universe where only love resides. It is a place of peace and learning. There is only love and joy here for you. People sometimes come here in their dreams, and some come when they die," replied the ancient one.

"Am I dead?" asked the girl.

The ancient one chuckled and said, "No, little one, you are spirit walking. You have come to the earth plane this time to be a healer and a woman of power. You will visit frequently with me here and in other universes as part of your teachings."

"Have I been here before?"

"Many times, in your dreams. Until you build enough personal power, you may not remember these trips, but the knowledge is there nonetheless. In a time of need, the knowledge will be there for you and you will wonder how you know it. We have been together many times in this and other lifetimes, little one," replied the ancient one.

"Why do I have no memory of it, Earth Mother?"

"Search your heart. Do you remember times of longing—a feeling of emptiness deep within your being that nothing seemed to fill, a feeling that you had a hole in your very being, a feeling of being alone even when you weren't? That was your love for me, that was your longing for your spiritual connection. It is a hunger that only the Goddess can fill. That is how you remember me at times. Where are those feelings now, little one?"

"They are gone. Ever since I can remember I have had a longing that words couldn't fully describe. I wish I had known that I was searching for you," said the girl.

The ancient one sighed and said, "I wish people knew that, too. As I have watched humanity over the centuries, I have seen much violence and suffering because of that longing. People seem willing to look for me only after they have looked everywhere else first. People try to fill that hole with other people, great wealth, power over others, and by staying so busy they have no time to feel. The list is endless and the cure is simple: merely learn to honor your spirituality."

"Why am I here? I am but a youngster," said the girl.

"Ah, little one, this is not your first life upon this planet. You ran out of places to look many lifetimes ago. This time you decided to remember early enough to make a difference in your life as well as the lives of others. You will be a light bearer and a great teacher in the years to come. It is time for you to go back now, little one."

"Not yet," shouted the little girl. "I just found you; I don't want to leave you ever again."

"You can't leave me, child. I live in your heart and in the heart of all beings. We will talk again soon, either in dream time or when you next spirit walk." The ancient one reached out and placed a beautiful crystal in the little girl's hand.

The little girl rubbed her eyes and smiled as she remembered her dream. Then she noticed the beautiful crystal in the palm of her hand and she knew that it wasn't a dream after all. She had found her way home at last.

Most humans seem to have a sense of longing at some time in their lives. After years of searching, I finally realized that what I longed for was connection with my soul. I looked "out there" for as long as I could, but to no avail. When I finally looked inside myself, I found the peace I longed for. I realized that the world was merely a mirror and that what I searched for resided deep within my being.

I have always been fascinated by mirrors. Years ago I owned a stained glass studio, and I made mirrors of different shapes and sizes with a variety of colorful designs around them. I also sold plants and gifts. There were hanging stained glass lamps floating in a sea of ferns, table lamps peeking from behind palm trees, all surrounded by sand castles. The store was very magical. I loved to stand behind the front counter and look at the store's reflection in the mirrors. If I looked just right, I could see an infinite number of stores getting smaller and smaller. I often wished that I could walk into that world. Little did I know that I would eventually get that opportunity.

Mirrors reflect our world and create an interesting perspective for us. There really is another world beyond the looking glass. A mirror is not only a metaphor for life, but it is also a doorway to your soul. Mirrors reflect what is going on in front of them, just as life reflects what is going on inside of you.

MIRROR WORK

Most people look in a mirror at least twice a day, yet they never truly see themselves. Years ago when I looked in the mirror, I always looked for blemishes or flaws. Were there any new wrinkles or pimples? I used mirrors to critique myself, and I was never kind or gentle. I am sure I would quickly lose friends if I said the same things to them that I said to myself while I was looking in the mirror.

One day I began consciously choosing what I said to myself in the mirror. I started telling myself that I was lovable, that I was perfect just the way I was. I began to tell myself gentle and loving things. At first my mind had a long list of what I call "Yeah, buts." I would say I was perfect and my mind would say, "Yeah, but you made a mistake," or "Yeah, but you're too fat"—the list was endless.

Slowly I became aware of the subliminal messages I had been repeating to myself for years. In a sense, those messages became self-fulfilling prophesies, because eventually I began to believe them and to live accordingly. As I began to counter those "Yeah, buts" with more positive messages, my life began to change. I started feeling better about myself and to believe that life could be good.

In my counseling practice, one of the first things I suggest to new clients is that they begin truly looking at themselves in the mirror. Almost everyone comes in the next week and sheepishly gives me a long list of excuses about why they didn't do the exercise. Mirrors are an amazingly powerful presence in our lives. Even people who love to look at themselves in the mirror seldom look directly into their own eyes. Try it for a moment: go into the bathroom and look deeply into one of your eyes. Take a few deep breaths, look deeply into that eye, and see what you see—what does it feel like? Are you even willing to put the book down and try it?

Next, talk to yourself. Say things out loud like, "I love myself, I accept myself, and I am perfect just the way I am." See how those words feel and what thoughts come to you as you say them. Ideally, begin doing this twice a day, first thing in the morning and before you go to bed. Talk to yourself for a few minutes each time and see what happens. If you feel foolish while you are doing this exercise or decide that you don't need to do it, then you really do need to do this exercise. If you do it and you feel neutral about it, then it will be no problem for you to continue. In other words, there is absolutely no valid excuse not to do this exercise. Practice doing it for at least one month.

Make a real effort to get comfortable looking at yourself in a mirror. Learn to love yourself and accept yourself the way you are. If you have body image issues, I suggest doing this exercise naked in front of a full-length mirror. Allow all the judgments you have about your body to rise up to the surface of your consciousness and counter them by saying something kind about yourself. These exercises are designed to help you release the critical judge that inhabits your mind. That voice does more to keep us stuck and unhappy than all the dysfunctional families and negative behaviors in the world combined.

Be gentle and loving with yourself. Take as much time as you need to get comfortable talking to yourself lovingly. If saying things like "I love myself" seems too far-fetched, say "I am learning to love myself." Make sure you can believe what you are saying to yourself. Remember feelings are not facts. Feeling foolish about doing this or thinking that this is a ridiculous exercise is not necessarily the truth. We often resist the very thing that is most important for our healing and growth.

MIRROR MEDITATIONS

Prior to the water initiation, Miguel had us meditate every morning and night as a group for about a month. It was an extremely moving and powerful experience. The group decided upon two times each day to meditate. The next morning when I sat down to meditate, I immediately felt the presence of the other group members. It felt like they were standing around me in a circle or a ring right there in my living room. My meditation was powerful, and emotions seemed to come out of nowhere. One moment I felt sad and the next furious.

That night I prepared to do my first mirror meditation. I had no idea what to expect, so at ten o'clock that night I nervously stood in front of my bathroom mirror with a candle and glass of water. I was not at all prepared for what I was about to see. As I stood there I felt the presence of the rest of the group and my protector.

After a few moments my face began to distort. First I saw blood flowing out of the corners of my eyes. Then I saw cuts and bruises all over my face. After a time the face looking at me from the mirror was no longer my own. As I looked around the room I began to see shadows on the walls that had no logical reason for being there. I was terrified. I really thought I was losing my mind. It was bizarre looking in the mirror and not recognizing the faces I saw.

I learned as I continued the process that meditating in front of a mirror was an opportunity to perform an emotional clearing. As time went on, I began to realize I was seeing events from past lives.

If you are working with a group, decide upon a convenient time each evening that you can meditate separately, but at the same time. My group found that just before retiring at night was a good time for us. This is a very important step toward finding your sacred center; make a commitment to the process. While my group was doing this form of meditation, people reported feeling the presence of the group even when they had forgotten that it was that time of day. One person sat in his car and used the rear-view mirror because he felt so compelled to follow through with the commitment. If you are doing this alone, still choose a specific time of day and stick to it.

You will need to get a candle and glass which you will use specifically for this process. A large mirror makes this process much easier and more interesting. You can stand or sit in front of the mirror but it is more comfortable if you can sit down.

Start by getting comfortable, lighting the candle, and placing a glass filled with water in front of you. You can place the candle on the right and the water on the left or the water on the right and the candle on the left—whichever you choose, be consistent. Call upon your protector and allow yourself to relax. With your eyes softly focused, look at yourself in the mirror. Focus your attention on breathing, allow it to become deep and rhythmic and relax your body. Allow yourself to go into a light meditative state with your eyes still open.

Watch the mirror and gently observe your face. While gazing softly at the mirror, look around the room and observe the shadows. Continue relaxing and observe what happens without judgment or any attempts to control the process. I suggest meditating for at least fifteen minutes.

At times this process may become very emotional. As much as possible allow the feelings to flow through you. If you feel sad, let yourself cry; if you feel angry, scream. Let yourself experience your emotions without becoming attached to them, simply let them flow. The main reason for this exercise is to release the emotional back log from the past, so try not to control or judge your emotions. So often we try to bottle our emotions. No matter how hard we try to ignore them, they are all still alive and well in our bodies somewhere. Those old emotions cripple our ability and limit our freedom of choice. In order to build our personal power we must free ourselves of the past. This is a wonderful way to do that.

Continue doing this meditation for a least a month, seven days a week. It may seem like a lot of work, but energetically we carry around old garbage with us anyway. As you watch yourself in the mirror, observe your thoughts. Watch them go and try not to follow them. You might write down your thoughts after each meditation, but, most importantly, let yourself feel whatever emotions come to you. Write letters, talk to people, yell, scream, holler—whatever is necessary to release those old feelings.

As you continue with this process, you may begin to get images from past lives. Treat them like any of your other thoughts: observe them. We often get so engrossed with our stories that we forget what we are doing or why we are doing it. This process is designed to clear out the past so your path to your sacred self, your spiritual essence, is not blocked. We must release any residual emotions and get to know ourselves. We are not the stories we endlessly repeat to ourselves, we are an energy that is infinite, immortal, and completely loving.

As we see things go by in the mirror, we begin to see that they are illusions and have no substance. At a physical level, we are more space than solid object. Our belief that we are solid is part of the illusion of this reality. The mirror is a wonderful tool. At one level it reflects our reality quite realistically. It is a wonderful place to begin seeing the illusions of this reality. "Out" there is an illusion, a mirror of our inner self. As we begin to see ourselves more clearly we will begin to see the world from a different perspective.

A ROOM OF MIRRORS

After my fire initiation, I helped Miguel complete the mirror room. It was a room about ten feet square with mirrors on all of the walls. It was an eerie feeling standing in the center of it. You could see an endless line of your reflections diminishing in size and moving off toward infinity. A mirror room is used to gain power and continue the process of letting go of the past and getting to know yourself better. You can make one fairly easily by buying four large framed mirrors and setting them together in a rectangle.

The first time I meditated in the room, one of my reflections suddenly stepped out of line and looked at me. At first I was startled, then fascinated. I found out a lot about myself during that experience.

If you have access to a large mirrored room (some dance studios have mirrors on all the walls), you can do any of the group meditations I discussed in Chapter Four. If you sit in a circle, it is best to sit facing directly toward the mirrors rather than looking at the mirrors through the group. As with the other mirror meditations, observe your thoughts and relax. Release your ideas about who you think you are, and let yourself find out more about who you really are.

EXERCISES

1. Continue writing about your personal myth. What is your story of your search for the holy grail? What is the meaning of life? What or who are you? What have you learned about yourself so far by doing these exercises? What is important to you? What meanings do you place on darkness, negativity, God, life, death, colors, and any other symbolism in your life?

2. Write letters to anyone in your life with whom you still have unfinished business or anyone close to you who has died. Write anything you need or want to say to them. If you feel angry, pour it out in a letter, say it all, release all your pent up feelings. Then forgive them for anything and everything you perceive that they have done to you. Ask them for forgiveness and forgive them. Communicate anything you wish you could have said to them. These are letters you will never mail. They are meant to assist you in achieving closure with those relationships. They will help set you free from the past. Be as thorough and emotional as possible.

3. When you are done writing the letters, create a ceremony to release yourself from that person and then burn the letters. Release any ties that bind you to those people. Set yourself free from the past. Let yourself step fully and clearly into the present.

4. What stories do you tell yourself and your friends most frequently? What are the themes of your stories? Are you frequently the victim? Is the world out to get you? Is life hard, or is it a joyous experience?

CHAPTER NINE

NATURE AND THE SENSES

The young woman had journeyed many miles and had many more to go. She had lost the trail days ago. She was exhausted, unsure if she could go on. The pines were tall and the wind whispered to her. She struggled on until she could walk no more. She slumped to the ground, oblivious to the softness of pine needles beneath her as she fell into a deep sleep.

She found herself walking in a wonderful forest, feeling strangely safe and loved. The air was sweet and clear. She heard voices everywhere, but she couldn't see anyone. She didn't feel frightened, only curious. She listened carefully and finally realized that one of the voices was coming from a tall tree nearby.

As she slowly approached, the voice stopped. She walked to the tree and began looking around it. There were no footprints and no one up in the tree branches. She was confused and a bit timid, but using her best power voice, she asked, "Who is there? Where are you? What do you want?"

A deep baritone voice said, "I think she can hear us."

"Of course I can hear you, but where are you? Why are you hiding from me?" asked the young woman.

Her statement was followed by a chorus of laughter. A gentle feminine voice said, "Obviously she can hear us, but she can't see us."

The baritone replied, "It has been so long since a human has listened to us; do you suppose she is safe?"

"Where are you?" shouted the girl.

"I am sorry; I am the spirit within the apple tree to your left—follow my voice. That's right," said the feminine voice.

As the girl walked and stood in front of the tree, it said, "Hello, I am pleased to meet you."

The young girl looked confused as she stood in front of the tree. "Was that really you talking?"

"Of course, who else could it be?" answered the tree. "I have heard legends about the days when humans were able to talk to nature, but I thought they were myths made up by the old ones.

"As a seedling I was told stories about humans and how they would talk to our spirits before they ate our fruits. The old ones told me to bless my fruit whenever the humans picked it, even though they didn't ask first. I asked the old one why the animals always asked us first if they could pick our fruit and humans never did. I could hear the humans talking to each other, and I wondered why they did not hear me.

"The old ones told me to have pity on the humans. They had forgotten about their spirits, so they could no longer hear ours.

"They told me that humans once lived in harmony with nature, but they had forgotten how. They said that it might appear at times that they are hurting us, but in truth they are the ones in pain."

"How is it I can hear you?" asked the young woman.

A short distance from the apple tree stood a magnificent oak tree that was hundreds of years old. It towered above the rest of the trees and many of its limbs were gnarled and twisted with age.

The apple tree said, "Why don't you talk to the old one over there? Be respectful if you want answers."

The girl walked over and stood in front of the old tree. She knelt down and in a subdued voice said, "Grandfather, I am honored to be in your presence. I never knew trees had spirits that could talk, and I apologize for my ignorance. I wish to honor you and understand what is happening now."

"Little one, you have listened well at the hearth of your teacher. She has taught you much, but now it is time for you to learn firsthand. Your body is asleep in your universe, and you have come to ours so that you may learn. Listen well, and if you are lucky, you will remember what you hear and bring great gifts to your people.

"All of nature is alive—every creature, every rock, every hill. Everything has a spirit and a soul. Nature will talk to you if you listen. But you must be very still and listen for the whispers. You must honor everything. You must never take anything without asking both the object and the spirit of the place.

"When you pick herbs for your healing, talk to them. Ask them if they are willing to leave their homes and merge their spirits with another so that a being may be healed. Stop to listen. Some plants are meant to be left behind so they can care for the land and the young ones who follow. Without the old ones' guidance, they might not remember the truth, and then they would be useless for healing.

"If you want to eat a plant or animal, honor its spirit, don't just take what you want. Give thanks for those that give up their lives that you may survive. Always walk upon the earth with your heart filled with love and gratitude. Open your heart so you can feel the love and protection that always surrounds you. Open your eyes so you can see—truly see—the world. Open your ears so you can hear all the magic around you. Listen for the whispers."

"But how, Grandfather? How?" asked the young woman.

"It is very simple," said the oak. "Open your heart—let yourself love. Love yourself and your world as fully as you can. Whisper into the wind if you need help or don't know how. Miracles happen when you stop being who you think you are and allow yourself to become who you really are. 'I don't know' is the key to your freedom. Once you empty yourself of the belief that you know who you are, you become an empty vessel, and then you are ready to receive the truth. Go in love, my child."

The young woman slowly began to stir and gradually opened her eyes. A lively chipmunk stood chattering in front of her. She was hungry and her entire body ached. "If only you could speak," she said out loud.

"But I can," said the chipmunk.

The girl slowly rubbed her eyes and shook her head. "I must be weaker than I thought," she mused. She stared into space for a moment trying to remember something. Then the girl smiled.

She sat up, took a deep breath, and whispered, "I don't know how, please help me."

Before I began studying with Miguel, I would have laughed at the idea of talking to nature. I was so out of touch with the world around me that I never felt the loving and gentle presence of nature. I was too busy living in my head. I wasn't sensitive enough to feel all the love that existed in nature. Sure, I'd admired a beautiful sunset or a spectacular view, but I never had stopped to feel the energy in them.

Nature is a wonderful teacher. It can be a gentle and loving guide on our paths toward self discovery. When I stand out in a gentle rain, walk along a beach, or stand in a forest, I feel a sense of serenity and peace. The wind is my ally or teacher; whenever I am in turmoil and I feel the wind, I immediately feel better. Early in my studies the wind began talking to me, not in words but on an emotional level. Whenever I feel the wind I remember that I am not alone. I once again feel connected and welcomed. The wind reminds me of my center when I am so caught up in my mind that I forget who I am and what is really important to me.

We tend to pay little attention to our environment unless it is uncomfortable or inconvenient in some way. I have the good fortune of living in Hawaii where the weather is almost always perfect. The trade winds gently caress the islands, keeping the temperature in the balmy eighties most of the year. I take it for granted that it will be another beautiful day in paradise. When it rains or the winds die down, I am much more aware of the elements.

When I lived in Vermont, I was painfully aware of the seasons. After a long gray winter I was overjoyed by the first signs of spring. As soon as the snow began to melt, my mood began to lighten and I would feel elated. Here in Hawaii the signs of spring are much more subtle. The trees lose their leaves in the spring and the plumeria trees look like scraggly twigs with beautiful flowers springing forth from their tips. When I noticed that the plumeria trees were in bloom the other day, I felt all the old feelings of spring fever rising to the surface even though I never felt cold or deprived of sun as I did in Vermont.

When I first felt elated, I wasn't sure why. After I saw the blooms on the plumeria, I realized I was excited because it was spring. Whatever we focus on and wherever we place our attention dictates what we experience in life. Today when I focus on the signs of spring, I experience excitement; when I was a teenager I loved skiing so I hated the signs of spring. Is the glass half empty or half full? If we concentrate our attention on what our minds tell us, our experience is very limited. As we expand our focus to include all of our senses, we also expand what we are able to experience.

In Chapter Six you did an exercise to help you become more sensitive to your physical senses. In a way you turned up the volume on your senses. Focusing on your senses is a wonderful way to quiet your mind. My mind tends to stay busy all the time; it seldom stops talking. When I expand my focus and notice the wind, I immediately lose track of my mind chatter. I am no longer focused on myself alone—I am in the moment and I feel better.

Whenever I connect with nature, I feel better. Nature is amazingly loving and immense. When I stand on the beach or on a mountaintop and look at the sky, I realize how insignificant my problems are. I am a tiny speck in this huge universe that is filled with love. Go out at night and watch the stars. One moonless night go outside and open up to the experience;

notice what happens to your sense of perspective. Listen to your heart instead of your mind for a few moments. Focus on nature and allow it to quiet your mind.

Nature will teach you if you get quiet enough to listen. It communicates with us whether we listen to it or not. Have you ever gone for a walk and felt yourself grow quieter or more peaceful? Nature constantly works with us on a core level. Our energy fields actually change as we are exposed to the gentle energy of nature or the ragged energy of a busy city. Our bodies relax and our minds become quieter in nature; we often experience stress in the city.

I have noticed that most people tend to talk in whispers when they go hiking in the forest. People seldom run around frantically or scream loudly. When people are in a forest, they tend to become quiet and solemn, as if they were in church. Most people seem to have a sense of reverence or awe as they walk through a forest. Trees give off a peaceful, quiet energy.

If you go out to the beach, however, you will often find people playing and laughing. The breaking waves give off a bubbly and light energy that tends to make human beings feel more playful. The energy of mountains vary, some make people want to yell while others make people feel humble. Our behaviors are affected by the energies around us. Nature can have a profound effect on our moods and our general state of well-being. We are seldom aware of the effect nature has on us, but it is there nonetheless.

Take a few minutes to stand next to a busy freeway or in the middle of downtown at rush hour and notice how your body feels. Next, go to a park or forest and listen to the sounds of nature for a few minutes. Do you notice any difference in the way you feel? If you get in touch with yourself you will feel entirely different. As you begin to focus on your environment you can use it as a tool. We can work in harmony with nature and allow it to assist us in our healing.

Working with nature is a matter of focusing our attention and having patience and dedication. An open mind also helps, because talking to trees, rocks, and plants does seem a little crazy to our minds. Nature communicates in many subtle ways, so you have to listen carefully.

TREES

Trees are a wonderful place to practice your "communicating skills." Trees are such a gentle yet powerful energy and almost everyone has easy access to them. Start by finding a tree that is somewhat secluded. It can be in the middle of a busy city, but it is easier to relax if you aren't afraid someone is watching you.

Once you have chosen a tree, stand in front of it. Greet it and thank the tree for its presence in your life. Honor the spirit of that tree and try to be open so you can let yourself sense it. Relax and breathe deeply. Imagine yourself talking to that tree. What would it have to tell you; what do you suppose it would want to share with you? How would it feel to talk to a tree?

As you stand in front of the tree, imagine that you are a tree. What would it feel like? Close your eyes and feel your roots going deep into the ground; sense the earth hugging your roots and supporting you. Feel your trunk as the sap slowly moves up from your roots carrying nutrients to your leaves. Feel the sun on your leaves and the wind gently caressing you. Allow yourself to feel rooted and supported. Imagine birds lovingly building nests and raising families in your branches. Breathe deeply and let yourself become a tree. What does it feel like? Watch life happening around you. What is your experience of time; what do you think about people? Relax and allow your consciousness to fall into the experience.

Slowly bring yourself back to normal consciousness. Take a deep breath and thank the tree for its help. Take a few minutes to write about your experience. Notice how the world looked from the perspective of a tree. What have you learned about yourself by being a tree?

Next, lean against the tree. Place your back against the tree and if possible stand barefoot. Place your head against the tree and ask it to share its energy with you. Thank the tree in advance for its healing and call upon the energy of the four directions: north, south, east, and west. Ask for their protection and guidance. Next call upon the earth, wind, fire, and water. Ask the elements to bless and guide you. Now relax.

You will begin to feel a gentle rocking within your body. It is subtle, but it definitely feels like you are slowly shaking back and forth, inside your body. Let the shaking continue. Relax and enjoy the energy as it flows through you. When the rocking stops, thank the tree and move away. Your body will feel a great deal lighter and more relaxed. Thank the tree for its healing and its love. If it seems appropriate, leave an offering for the tree's spirit. You could leave cornmeal or seeds or anything natural that is appropriate.

Visit the tree on a regular basis if you can. Do this exercise with a wide variety of trees. Notice if broadleaf trees feel differently to you than fir trees. Notice if the same type of tree feels differently in various locations or as the seasons change. Practice being more sensitive to nature in general.

WEATHER

Have you ever known someone who said they could always tell when it was going to rain? Can you notice changes in the weather before they happen? Years ago Native Americans could forecast the weather by the signs. They lived in harmony with nature so they were aware of the subtle changes that take place before the weather shifts. In many areas of the world the changes in season are quite dramatic.

When I lived in California, the changes in the seasons were subtle. In the winter the sky was a little bluer and the winds felt different. It was quite a bit cooler, and the ocean also changed colors. After a time I could sense when the rains were coming.

Most people laugh when I tell them that there is a change of seasons in Hawaii. Each year I live here the changes become more obvious to me. Some changes are easy to note: the trade winds are not as consistent in the winter, and it rains more often. Some of the changes are more subtle: the color of the sky, the movement of the birds, and the smell of the air are all signs of a change in the weather. Some people can become sensitive enough to feel the change of barometric pressure.

Noticing the subtle changes in the weather and being able to read those signs is a matter of practice. When I lived in Vermont, I could always tell when a thunderstorm was coming because the leaves on the trees changed color.

Observing the weather and noticing the patterns will help you build your sensitivity to nature and the various energies in our universe. It will help in many areas of your life if you let it. Nature is a powerful force, and as you become more sensitive to it, you can better use its loving presence in your life.

It was an awesome experience when hurricane Iniki came through the islands. For several days before the storm arrived, the air felt heavy and strangely still, even though the wind was blowing. A few of the older inhabitants said it felt like hurricane weather. As the storm approached, the island became oddly silent and still. Even the birds fell silent. The storm itself was devastating. One minute everything was calm, and a few hours later roofs were blowing off. The next day the sun was out and everything was calm again. You would never have known a hurricane had been through except for the downed power lines, the houses without roofs, and the trees stripped of their leaves by the winds.

Experiencing the fury and raw power of nature was humbling and inspiring. The next time a thunderstorm comes through your area, go out and feel its energy. Make sure you find a safe place, where you can sit and allow yourself to "feel" the storm.

One of the most profound experiences I ever had was watching a thunderstorm late one night as a teenager in Vermont. We lived in a valley at the foot of a mountain, so the storms often spent the night rattling up and down the valleys. This storm was particularly violent, and it woke me up. My bedroom was upstairs, and I watched out my window as the sky lit up every few minutes. There were large sugar maple trees in front of the house, and the wind was violently whipping through them. As I watched the fury of that storm, I was struck by the thought that there had to be more to life than my physical existence. At that instant, I saw the face of the Great Spirit in the storm.

One of the many gifts my mother gave me was my love of thunderstorms. Many people fear them; my grandmother was terrified of them because her cousin was killed by lightning while she was standing next to her. Storms are a wonderful time to release old feelings or to tap into raw power and use the energy for healing yourself or others. The air feels fresh and clean after a thunderstorm. The lightning makes the air smell alive. If you have crystals, you can charge them by placing them out in a storm.

When you feel a storm approaching, you can call upon the thunder beings and ask for their assistance. You can ask them to cleanse and release any negativity. You can ask them to teach and guide you. As you become more sensitive to their energy, they will show you how to work with them.

Take time to observe the weather patterns in your area. How do you feel when it rains or before or after a storm? Notice any internal changes and see if you can link them to changes in the weather. Notice the subtle changes during the day. How does the sun hit your room; how does it look before a rain or after the sun comes back out? Make nature and the weather your friend. Play in the rain. Watch the clouds. Observe how you can live in harmony with that energy.

WIND

I have always loved the wind; it is magical to me. As a child, I loved flying kites and watching clouds as the wind whipped them along. At night, I loved listening to the leaves in the tree that was outside my bedroom window. When I began my studies with Miguel the wind began to talk to me. At first I thought I was crazy, but the wind has pulled me out of an emotional funk more than once. One day as I was sitting outside my apartment in San Diego, I found myself obsessing about a problem. I was getting more and more upset. Suddenly the wind came up and began to swirl around me. I heard a gentle voice reminding me that this world is an illusion and suddenly the problem lost all of its power.

If you would like to have the wind as an ally, begin by getting to know it. Spend time outside, relaxing in the wind. Listen to the shadows in the sound of the wind. Listen to the wind and notice how it moves over the earth. Invite it into your life and begin talking to it as you would a friend. Begin to notice how the wind feels on your body and see if you can tell the difference between male and female winds. See if you can tell where the wind has been.

Find a place to meditate where you can feel the wind on your skin. Open up to it, feel its presence, and let yourself know that it has consciousness. Ask the wind to teach you about itself. Surround yourself with an energy of flexibility and let yourself become one with the wind. Let your consciousness travel with the wind as it moves over the earth. Imagine yourself as a molecule of air and float with the wind.

The wind is like life; it is an illusion. It has no substance of its own, yet it is pure energy. It is simply a force that makes the air move. Imagine yourself as pure energy, as the force that makes your life move. Let the wind teach you. Relax and allow your partnership with the wind to unfold in its own manner.

WATER

Water is a very healing and cleansing element. It covers most of the surface of this planet, and our bodies are composed mainly of the substance. This is truly the water planet. Each body of water has its own personality and unique feeling. For the purpose of these exercises, I have divided water into two major groups: streams (moving water), and oceans or lakes (still water).

STREAMS

Streams are wonderfully relaxing and a great place for doing release work. They are inhabited by a variety of friendly water spirits. Waterfalls and rapids are high energy places to meditate. As with any element of nature, it is a matter of opening up and becoming aware of the spirits or energy. They've always existed, yet we have never taken the time to notice them. Water nymphs tend to be playful and mischievous. Give yourself time to become acquainted with them. Let them teach you about themselves. Approach them with an open mind and humility.

As with the wind, invite them into your world. Ask the energies to teach you. Meditate near the water; open your mind and relax. You will be amazed at the worlds you have been unaware of all these years. Rapids, babbling brooks, and lazy rivers all have different energies; let them talk to you. Rivers and streams have stories to tell. They can teach you about yourself if you are receptive and open to receiving information.

OCEANS AND LAKES

The ocean tends to be a little less playful than streams. The waves have powerful and playful beings in them. The shadows in the waves also contain a door to the ethereal realms. It is restful and insightful to sit by the ocean and write or meditate. Free yourself from your inhibitions and act like a child again. Invite the waves to toss you and let yourself laugh and play in them. Ask the ocean or the lake to teach you. Ask for its help and love. Playing in the waves is healing and nurturing. Let yourself surrender to the experience. Gently float on the surface of the water and let it support you. Let yourself feel its love. Let it talk to you.

ROCKS AND CRYSTALS

Rocks, large or small, are fun. I often find rocks that intrigue me while I am walking. If I sense that the rock wouldn't mind relocating, I take it home with me. Then, whenever I feel like it, I will meditate with it. Rocks have different personalities, some are stodgy and others are playful. Each one has a story, because they have been around for centuries.

There are a number of excellent books on the market about crystals and their uses. I suggest using your intuition when relating to crystals or stones. As you become more sensitive, it will be easy to hear the stones talking to you. Listen, ask them where they have been, and what they have experienced. If you let them, rocks can be informative.

One of my power spots in California was on the edge of a steep rock cliff. The power there was amazing; it energized me. I felt at one with the forces of the universe there. Explore natural rock walls or cliffs in your area. Stand in front of a tall natural rock cliff and do the same exercise you did with a tree.

PLANTS

Plants and I "talk" to each other. When I owned a plant store I would tell my employees that a plant had its hand up, which meant it needed water. They would proceed to tell me that they had just watered everything, and I had found the one small plant in the corner they had missed; I had heard it crying for water. Years ago a group of scientists experimenting with plants found that a plant "fainted" if brine shrimp were put in a pot of boiling water near them. The plants would also faint if the scientists *threatened* to kill the shrimp in their presence.

Find a quiet place and sit with a plant. Place your hands gently on its leaves and see if you can feel the life energy flowing through it. Buy a plant and spend time taking care of it. Try to sense when it needs water or if its pot is too small.

In order to work with nature we must increase our sensitivity and expand our definitions. All of nature has consciousness; we are simply unaware of the ways in which it communicates. Take time exploring the world in which you live.

EXERCISES

1. Notice how the time span varies as you connect with the various forms of nature. A rock's life span may be centuries, so its concept of time is very different from a plant that may live only a season. Spend time viewing your life using a plant's concept of time. How does that change the importance of the events happening in your life?

2. How does your emotional state vary as you explore nature? Do you feel better when you spend time with trees or the wind? Which element seems most relaxing to you? Each person has a specific element that is their ally. Which one is yours?

3. What area of this planet calls you? Do you feel more at home by the water, in the mountains, or in the desert? Do you feel safe in the country or do you need the distractions of the city? How do you feel about your neighborhood?

4. Practice talking to plants both indoors and outdoors in nature. Notice how each type of plant has a different personality. Let them really talk to you and be ready to listen carefully.

▲▲▲ CHAPTER TEN ▲▲▲

POWER

He had searched the world most of his life for power. He had gone to every known power spot, climbed every mountain, and sat before many teachers, but they had all failed him. His lungs were beginning to ache from the strain of climbing so high.

He remembered a time many years ago at the beginning of his search when he went out to the desert with an old Indian named Sunny. They had climbed to a peak at the end of an old arroyo. The man had heard that in ancient times it had been a powerful gathering place for medicine men. Sunny had asked him why he was going there. He had looked at the old man condescendingly and told him he was gathering power. Sunny had smiled oddly and told the man he already had all the power he ever needed.

Sunny had gone on to tell the man a child's tale about the dangers of power. A medicine man who lived many years ago also had gone off in search of power. He had left his tribe without a healer because he was obsessed with being the most powerful medicine man there ever was. He searched the land over for many years. He learned much, but it was never enough; there was a fire in his soul that nothing seemed able to extinguish. The more he searched, the more he was driven.

When he was old, he finally returned to his tribe, proud of his powers. In his absence, one of his young apprentices had become a healer. This young woman was loving, gentle, and kind. She was forced to learn her skills quickly when a plague had struck the village. The tribe loved her very much.

When the old medicine man strutted into the village, the Chief immediately called the tribe together. The medicine man put on his best clothing, expecting to be honored. He stood behind the Chief in his old place of power when the medicine woman entered. She nodded at the Chief and gently asked the medicine man to move aside. He bristled and asked her if she had forgotten who he was.

The Chief raised his hand and answered, "We have not forgotten who you are: a healer who deserted his tribe for his selfish ends. You are no longer welcome at our hearths. Go."

He began to argue, but everyone turned their backs on him and left. At first, he was going to place a curse upon the tribe, but then he remembered his old teacher. The teacher had told him that the world is a mirror, and he saw suddenly that they were only mirroring his own behavior. He had filled himself with power instead of love. He had lost the most valuable thing in the world.

The man remembered that upon finishing this tale, Sunny had asked him what tribe *he* had deserted.

Now Sunny and his story were in the past, and the man had traveled the world and was finally at the gate to the temple. He had heard tales about this place and how only the most devout people would be able to find it. He was very pleased with himself. Here was one more example of how powerful he was. He rang the giant gong and waited.

After what seemed like hours, an ancient monk came out and asked him what he wanted. He looked at the man with disdain and said, "I am here to see the Master."

The old man opened the gate and motioned for him to enter. He took the man into a room that was simple yet elegant. In the middle of the room was a low table with pillows placed around it for chairs. In the center of the table was a beautiful purple orchid in a shiny black pot. Outside of the large window was a low bench with several Bonsai plants on it. The tiny oak's leaves were showing their fall colors. Beyond, the view of the valley was breathtaking.

While the man surveyed the room, the old man returned with tea. The man thanked him but said, "Old man, I want to see the Master, not drink tea with you. I have searched the world for power and teachers of the truth. They have all failed me, and I have no time for such foolishness."

"One always has time for tea. Sit," said the old man gently.

There was something about the old man's voice that made him sit. He settled down on a pillow. He felt strangely relaxed as he held his cup for the old man to fill.

The old man slowly began to pour tea into the man's cup and as he did, he started to tell him a story about truth.

"People are often so busy worrying about themselves that they walk right by the teacher. The truth is always right in front of us if we get quiet enough to listen. . ."

The old man's voice seemed to drift off and the man found himself lost in watching the tea flow into his cup. He could not move. Slowly the tea began spilling over the edge of the cup and still the man could not move. The man watched, transfixed, as the tea poured slowly over the entire table. He finally jumped out of his seat when the hot liquid spilled over his legs.

He glared at the old man and asked, "What is wrong with you, old man? Are you crazy?"

The old man smiled and said, "In order to fill a cup with tea, you must start with an empty cup." And then he looked deeply into the man's eyes.

In that instant the man saw his life pass before him. He had always been so full of himself that he could not learn. The teachers had not failed him; he had failed himself. It was never power he sought, it was love. He needed the love so he would feel safe enough to surrender himself.

A tear slowly rolled down his check as he humbly said, "Master, I am sorry. Please help me, for I now realize that I know nothing."

The old man smiled and said, "The universe has been waiting a long time to hear that, my son. Now you can finally let the truth in."

Sunny had not been crazy after all, thought the man.

Often we think our answer or our happiness is right over the next hill. We think we know what will make us happy. We know that all we need is the right lover, job, house, or.... We search endlessly and are unwilling to admit we don't have a clue what would really make us happy.

Many times in the course of my studies I have struggled to get something, only to fail. In time I realized that I had been going in the wrong direction all along. If I had gotten what I had been seeking, I would have been miserable.

One day I went out to the desert with an old Indian. I told him I was looking for power. He laughed and told me I was already powerful. I now know that was true; what I was lacking was self-esteem and the ability to love myself. I thought more power would make me happy, when all I needed to do was love myself more.

Power is seductive, and it can also be a harsh task master. One of the many definitions of power is that it is an energy, force, or momentum. It is also defined as control over an object. I think of power as the ability to act or as a concentration of energy. I have learned to be extremely centered and focused whenever I handle a great deal of power because it is too easy to get lost in its grandeur. There is an illusionary quality about power that can fool us into believing that we can control things, that we can step out of harmony with our sacred selves and play God. It is only an illusion and a path that eventually leads to a great deal of pain and emptiness.

Avoid the allure of using power for your selfish ends at any cost. Use it only to strengthen your connection with your spiritual center. Learn to work in harmony with power, but never attempt to control it. Remain centered and act as a conduit or channel for its healing properties. Feel its loving presence and honor it. Ask it how you can be of service and do whatever you feel guided to do.

Learning to work with power is a wonderful way to accelerate your evolution. Use caution as you explore power and allow it to teach you. Remain a humble channel rather than attempting to be its master. Avoid the dark side of the force and remain always in the light.

POWER POINTS

Scattered over the surface of of an individual's aura are various power points. These points are areas where a person's energy varies in density or form, appearing either thicker or thinner than the rest of his or her energy field. Energy can be channeled into these points so the person can experience healing or have his or her consciousness pushed into another reality.

The human aura is actually a complex web of energy fibers. Power points are areas where these fibers intersect or join. By manipulating these points you can rearrange the fibers to adjust the person's energy field. Moving these fibers can change the person on an emotional, spiritual, or physical level. This in turn can heal a person of physical diseases or emotional turmoil. It can also bring him or her closer to the sacred self.

In this section we will learn how to recognize these power points. As with any of the techniques in this book, learning how to sense power spots will take patience and diligence. It is something we learn to do intuitively, not intellectually. You will have to work with a partner. One person should sit comfortably in a chair while the other person practices locating that person's power points.

To locate your partner's power points, stand behind the person and relax. Allow yourself to go into a light meditative state. As much as possible release your mind. In order to feel another person's power points, you must see with your spiritual eyes. When you see with your spiritual eyes, you don't *see* as much as *feel;* you sense at a deep level of your being. After you are relaxed, slowly begin to move your hands over the other person's body, being sure to not touch the body.

Place your hands about six inches from the body and notice how it feels. Place all of your attention on the area between your hands and the person's body. Close your eyes and breathe deeply; let your mind relax. What do you see, and what can you sense?

Allow your hands to become sensitive to the temperature and texture of the person's body. Move your hands in and out as well as over the surface of the body's energy field. Stay relaxed and breathe deeply. Don't try too hard. Simply allow yourself to feel, really feel from deep within your being. Instead of thinking with your head, feel with your heart. Ask the universe for help in sensing this person's power points, and let your sacred self guide you.

At first, as you move your hands over a certain spot you may sense a strange pulling or tugging at your hands. This is a power point. It may feel like a slight shift in temperature. A particular spot may feel warmer or cooler. Certain areas may feel sluggish or sticky or you may feel static electricity. Allow yourself to be sensitive to any change in sensations. Trust your inner knowing. Don't debate with your mind. If you think it is a power point, it is a power point.

Once you find a point, ask the person how it feels as you move your hand over it. Without touching the individual, ask him or her where you are working. Both of you can then build the sensitivity. Take turns practicing until you can easily locate at least several points on each other. The location of the power points varies from person to person, and from one day to another.

Be patient with yourself. Learning how to feel and sense on these levels is a new experience for your mind. You have been trained most of your life to filter out any information you receive from these levels. When you learned to walk as a child, you fell down often. If you had given up or been impatient with yourself, you would still be in your crib or be crawling around on your hands and knees. Be patient with yourself! Let yourself learn how to walk through these new levels. Have fun and enjoy the process.

POWER SPOTS

Just as human beings have power points, the earth also has areas where its energy varies. These are called power spots. Places like Stonehenge and the Valley of the Dead are examples of power spots. Just as human beings have areas where their energy is more concentrated, so does the earth. Most of the older churches and temples were built on power spots, where it is much easier to connect with the spiritual realms. When you approach a sacred place, you can feel its power and the strength that lies there. These places can be used to intensify your personal power and to assist you in connecting more fully with your spiritual center.

Whenever you enter a room you automatically gravitate toward a place that feels comfortable. The place that you feel most comfortable is often your personal power spot. It is the place that balances most closely with your own energy. As you stand or sit in this spot, your energy is magnified; it is like putting jumper cables on a car battery.

The ability to consciously find these power spots can greatly enhance your sensitivities to energy and your own process. Being able to find these spots is like many of the other exercises in this book; they all allow you to know a little more about yourself than you did before.

I suggest you find your power spot in nature. In any given location, there is a place that fits you better energetically than any other location. There are also places that can drain your energy and make you feel and act less effectively. It is important to be able to tell the difference. One spot may energize you while another weakens you and can actually make you sick.

There are three major types of power spots. One type gives you energy and is healing. Another type of spot actually drains energy from anything within its boundaries. There are also power spots that are tricksters. They confuse people and trick them into giving up their power or sanity. It takes practice to be able to differentiate between them. The easiest way to tell the difference between the types is by how you feel. It is important to trust how you feel and what you sense as you explore the energy levels of the different types of power spots. These spots affect you whether you are consciously aware of them or not.

Begin by calling upon your protector and ask the universe for guidance. Relax and focus on your breathing. Slowly look around the area. Does one spot "look" brighter than the others? See how each section feels as you stand in it. Feel from your heart. Do some feel lighter and some heavy? Do you feel confused as you stand in some places? Now slowly walk around the area. Take time to stand in any place that attracts you. Compare how each one feels to you. Notice the plants and grasses in the various areas. Do they look healthier in one place, greener and more alive? Let yourself know intuitively where your power place is.

Now sit down and begin to meditate. How do you feel as you sit in that spot? Does the energy feel loving and peaceful? If it feels rough or unsettling, move. Soon it will become second nature; you will automatically sit in your power spot. Avoid listening to your mind during this process. My mind still suggests that the spots I choose are wrong. Trust that inner knowing. Your inner knowing, your sacred self, will never lie to you.

When I lived in California, I had a power spot in the mountains that I visited frequently. The view of the desert was spectacular and the winds intense. This spot literally called to me. The day I found it I was going to the mountains to do a ceremony. At first I drove by, but I felt compelled to go back. I walked up the mountain and sat transfixed for hours. After that, I periodically would feel called to go to visit that spot. Whenever I went, I received a gift of some sort. Power spots are sacred, they can add greatly to the quality of our lives.

POWER MOVES

Power moves are movements that we make with our bodies that assist us in concentrating and directing the energy. Most martial arts use power moves to one degree or another. When people dance from their hearts, they are doing power moves, allowing the power to speak through their bodies. Power moves are a dance of power. Tai Chi is an ancient example of power moves.

Whenever you handle energy, you receive it with your left hand and send it with your right hand. Your left hand acts as an antenna and your right hand broadcasts the energy you have received. If you are open to its direction, power will instruct you—it will "tell" you what to do. Flowing with that energy can be a powerful and centering experience. It can also be distressing when you fight it or try to control it.

This dance of power begins as you relax and become mentally centered. Stand quietly with your legs shoulder-width apart. Mentally give the power permission to flow through you and ask it to guide you. Raise your hands and hold them in front of you. Let your hands and body move as you feel guided. Your movements will be smooth and rhythmic, almost like ballet.

Power moves are a form of moving meditation. They are relaxing and energizing. As you do them, you collect a great deal of power in your body. They are healing to both mind and body. If it feels appropriate, you can play gentle music or light a candle. Relax and let the energy move your body. Notice how it feels as it flows through you. After you have relaxed into the energy, allow it to move you for about fifteen minutes and then stop. Gently sit down and close your eyes. Ask the universe how to use the energy you have collected. If you don't get a specific answer, send the energy to Mother Earth so it can heal the planet, yourself, and the people you love. Allow yourself to bathe in the joy of that energy.

After I do power moves, I usually feel relaxed and loved. I feel connected to the source and centered. The more I surrender to that energy, the more complete the healing is. It is such a wonderful way to get out of our normal, everyday consciousness and move into an altered state. At first I felt foolish standing and moving around randomly, but now I enjoy it so much I hardly notice my mind's negative commentary.

If you are having a difficult time feeling the guidance of that energy, start with your hands. Hold them in front of your face and move your right hand clockwise and your left hand counter-clockwise. Move them slowly and rhythmically in and out. Gently notice how it feels. Then while you are sitting in a chair, begin moving your legs in a circular motion, noticing how it feels.

After you are comfortable with those movements, stand up and again begin with your hands. First move one hand out and away from you and then step rhythmically out with one of your legs. Next do the same thing with the other hand and leg. Slowly begin moving around the room. Notice your body and let yourself enjoy its movements. Allow the process to be sensual and rhythmic. Be gentle with yourself as you practice allowing your awareness to expand. Enjoy the process.

If you have the opportunity, watch Native American dancers, Sufi dancers, or any aboriginal tribal dances. These are all excellent examples of power moves. As you watch, let yourself sense the power as it builds.

INITIATIONS

Initiations are one of the many ways power can be used. Traditionally, initiations occur at various times in the life of a spiritual seeker. Baptism is an example of an ancient initiation. It was believed to be a time when the child was infused with the presence or spirit of God.

When I studied with Miguel, he conducted a series of initiations. They were beautiful ceremonies in which he imparted power to each of the students. He actually changed each of the participants energetically. After each initiation we were able to handle more power than before. In an initiation there is always a power person, or someone who knows how to impart power.

The actual events of the ceremony are irrelevant; it is the intention to impart power that is important. If you feel ready to do an initiation for your group, let your inner voice be your guide.

A water initiation can be an empowering experience. Have one person act as the leader, or if you honor a particular spiritual leader, ask him or her to help your group. Take care in choosing the leader because it is a big responsibility.

Once you have chosen a leader, decide upon a location. It could be by a body of water or indoors. Have everyone dress completely in white. You will need to construct an altar of some sort, and include a few candles and a large shell or wooden container to hold the water.

When the setting is prepared, have all the participants sit in a circle in front of the altar and go into a light meditative state. The leader should go into a light trance and open the ceremony with a prayer. It could sound like this:

> *Great Spirit, Universe, Oh Mighty Creator, we come before you to honor your spirit and to move closer to you. We ask your blessing on our gathering, and I ask to be a channel for your love and wisdom. I humbly ask to be a conduit to impart a greater degree of wisdom, power, and commitment to those who come before us. Please guide me and direct me.* (As the leader says the prayer, he should light the candles on the altar.)

The leader should take a few moments to get centered and to open up to the energy. Then, one by one, each of the participants should stand before him. The leader then asks them what they are willing to commit to, what they wish to receive, and to open up to the love of the Creator. The leader pours water over their heads (it only needs to be a few drops). After everyone has come forward, the leader says a simple prayer of thanksgiving and then blows out the candles. The prayer can be as simple as:

> *Thank you, oh Creator, for honoring us with your love and your presence. We give thanks and offer ourselves as instruments of your love and healing. In love and light we give thanks.*

Whenever you conduct a ceremony in a particular place, you create a power spot. By doing this ceremony, you have created a sacred place. Use it wisely.

EXERCISES

1. Practice finding power spots wherever you go.

2. Find your special power spot. We all have places on this earth that are sacred to us. Take time to find your sacred place. Once you find it, spend some time there. Let that place heal you and fill you with its love. Let your heart guide you to that place. It will call you if you are willing to listen.

3. Buy a packet of seeds and divide it in half. Do some power moves and then sit quietly with half of the seeds. Allow yourself to feel their life energy and then slowly begin channeling energy to them. Mentally see them growing big and strong. Plant each group of seeds in separate pots and give them equal care. Notice how much healthier the energized group is.

CHAPTER ELEVEN

HEALING

The chill in the air seemed heavier than before. Her old bones ached with the cold. She poked at the fire and added another log. Her days were almost over. She would be sad to leave the little ones, but she would be with them in spirit, and at least her body would no longer ache. She took another sip from her herbal tea. It barely eased the pain these days. She nodded off to sleep and when she awoke, the children were all gathered at her feet. They loved surprising her.

"I am sure your mothers would be happy if you were half as quiet in the morning. Welcome, my friends," said the woman.

A chorus of little voices said, "I love you, Grandmother."

She reached into her pocket and gave the children some treats. As they passed them around, she began her story.

"Once, many years ago, our people were very sick. The Great Spirit looked down upon them and felt sad. He asked Brother Bear what he could do to help the people.

"Bear said, 'My people know what plants to eat when they feel sick. The strong ones get well after they eat the plants. The mother takes time to teach the young which plants to eat and which to avoid.'

"The Great Spirit thought about this and said, 'I must remind the people about the gift plants have to offer. I must also remind them of the power my love has to heal. It would take too long to teach all the people. Perhaps we could train one of them and that one could teach others.'

"The Bear and the Great Spirit thought this was a good idea so they searched among the people to find a suitable student. The Bear suggested they teach the candidate during dream time. At last they found a woman who was promising.

"They realized that they would have to get the people to trust her before they could teach her about herbs. There were taboos about eating many plants that were the most healing. They decided to teach her about energy healing first.

"The first night they called to the woman and told her that she had a wondrous power within her. She had the power to heal her people. When she awoke from her dream she was afraid. What power could she possibly have? As she felt their love night after night, she began to feel safe and have the courage to acknowledge her gifts. Each night they instructed her on the power of love. They taught her how to call upon the powers of the Great Spirit and to channel that energy through herself safely.

"After they had been instructing her for about a month, one of the little ones fell and hurt herself. Her arm was broken, and she was bleeding severely. The woman rushed to her side, knelt down and said the prayer she had learned in her dreams. She held the child in her arms and prayed quietly in the manner she had been taught. She held her hands over the wound and the bleeding stopped. She gently rocked the little girl back and forth and rubbed her arm. As she did, the bone mended. She felt so tired that she fell asleep with the little girl still in her arms.

"When she awoke, several of the women were gathered around her with amazement and fear on their faces. The child's mother was standing with tears in her eyes. She asked the woman how she had healed her little girl. The woman told them of her dreams and was relieved to finally share her secret. She told how the Great Spirit visited her with the Bear each night and taught her about healing.

"Not everyone was convinced that this power came from the Great Spirit, but as time went by the doubters became believers. After a time, the woman also learned how to call upon the energies of nature to help with the crops and animals. Life became easier and more joyous for the people.

"Her lessons continued for a long time until she was able to talk to nature and the spirits herself. She learned about the healing powers of plants. She learned to honor all of nature and to walk softly upon the earth. In the last lesson she was told to teach others and to share her gifts with anyone who would listen. She had come to love her teachers and asked if other people could have teachers as well. The Great Spirit smiled and said that they already did."

The old woman again focused on the room and the intent faces of the children sitting at her feet. Oh, how she would miss the little ones.

Every culture has had healers. Their respective roles and status in the community varied, but generally they were highly regarded. In truth, we heal ourselves with our faith. When we go to a healer, we believe they can heal us, so they do. The ability to heal lies within each of us, we merely have to activate it.

My first experience with psychic healing happened while I was still living in Vermont. One bitter winter day I tried to start my car without my gloves on. I had left the keys in the ignition and it was thirty degrees below zero. Almost immediately I froze the tips of several of my fingers and thumb. When they thawed out, I was in a great deal of pain so I went to the doctor; he told me that they were badly frostbitten. He said he doubted if the feeling would return in the tips of my fingers. I made my living working with my hands, so I was very upset.

A few weeks later I went to see a woman who was a well-known psychic and an excellent healer. She grasped my hand and let out a loud squeal. She held my numb fingers in her hands for a few minutes and gently talked to me. She told me my hands would be fine. Later that day the feeling returned to my fingers and the next day a very thick layer of skin peeled off. Would my fingers have done that anyway? I will never know, but I am convinced that it was Jeanne's healing touch and my faith in her that cured them.

We have all come here to heal ourselves, each other, and the planet. When I first moved to California I went to a spiritualist church where a healing service was held each week. I was interested in healing so I began studying with several people. That interest is what led me to Sister Sarita. She was well-known throughout southern California for her healing skills.

Perfection is our natural state of being. Whenever any disharmony or disease exists in our bodies or lives, we can easily release it by stepping back into harmony with our sacred selves. Anything less than perfection is an illusion, but when I am sick I can certainly ignore that fact. Spiritual healing is a wonderful way to remind ourselves of our perfection. One of my teachers told me that my job as a healer is to see people in their perfection and mentally remind them so they can let go of the disharmony.

I see healing as a way that we can share love with one another. When I am performing a healing on someone, it feels like I am channeling a loving energy. Healing is not something I do; it is a process I allow to happen through me. I step out of the way and allow that healing energy to channel through me. The more completely I step out of the way, the more effective I am as a healer. A successful healing does not necessarily mean that the person gets rid of the disease. When I work with AIDS patients, sometimes the healing takes place when they have made peace with themselves and their world. When a person dies, it doesn't mean the healing wasn't successful; it means that he or she was done on this planet.

The first night I came home from a healing class I was so excited I decided to practice on my dog. She didn't like that idea. When I started channeling energy into her, she ran away. I later learned that animals tend to be sensitive to this energy. When you work on them you have to turn down the volume.

There are hundreds of different ways to perform spiritual healing. I have found that these differences are mainly of style rather than substance. Eventually, everyone develops their own style, their own way of performing healings, their own way to act as channels for the healing energy. Unfortunately there are a large number of people who prey on people's desperation and pain. Beware of healers who are more than willing to tell you how wonderful they are. Truly spiritual healers are humble. I know that my ability to act as a channel for that healing energy is a gift that I must honor and nurture. If I allow my ego to use that gift, it will dissipate.

The guidelines I will give you on how to heal are just that: guidelines. As you practice, you will develop your own style. There are beings of light that will help you. They will work through you and assist you in performing healings. All you have to do is ask them for help and give them permission to work with you.

Over the years, I have worked with a wide variety of styles and a large number of props. At various times, I have worked with pure energy, herbs, and aromatherapy. I now use a combination of all three as well as anything else that works. Let your intuition be your guide. During the course of my studies, I found myself becoming interested in various subjects. For a period of time, I would read everything on a particular subject I could find. Then, just as suddenly as the interest arose, it would leave, and I would be reading about another subject. Let your intuition and your interests guide you in your reading and in your selection of teachers.

HANDS-ON HEALING

When Sarita performed a healing, she would go into a trance and begin channeling healing energy. She called this process "putting on her protector." She would start by saying a prayer and then she would cleanse the person's aura. What happened next would be guided by the energy and the person's complaint.

She often performed psychic surgery, which is beyond the scope of this narrative to teach. Psychic surgery is a profound form of spiritual healing in which the healer literally cuts into the recipient's body. She did this without drawing blood. Traditional psychic surgery is a bloody process. She believed that making people bleed was unnecessary and called it show-boating. She said that the blood did help convince people that the healer was doing something, but it was totally unnecessary.

Faith and the person's belief system play a large part in any form of healing, even in traditional medicine. Unless the patient has faith in the doctor, the chances of being cured are not very great. Healing occurs when people change their perspectives. At some level the individuals once again see themselves as healthy, and then they are.

You can learn how to heal by working alone in your meditations. While you are meditating, ask for guidance and help in becoming a channel for healing energy. There are light beings that will work with you whenever you perform a healing. I am not aware of the names or descriptions of the beings that work with me when I heal, but I can feel their presence.

MEETING YOUR HEALERS

You can do a ceremony to assist yourself in connecting with your healers. I find it useful to set aside time to connect with those energies. You can begin by smudging the area and lighting a candle. Next say a prayer and ask the universe for assistance before going into the meditation.

You could say something like:

> Universe, Great Spirit, Creator, I come before you as
> your humble servant. I wish to be made a channel for your
> healing energy and your love. I know that there are beings
> of light that are willing to assist me on this quest. I ask for
> their assistance and your guidance. May I be made a clear
> channel for your healing energy, and may I always remain

*a humble servant to that energy. I ask that those beings of
light come to me now that I may get to know them. May I
be receptive to their teachings, and may I learn how best to
work with them. So it has been asked for, so it will be
received. I give thanks.*

MEDITATION

*Allow yourself to relax. Breathe deeply and open up your head and
your heart. As you inhale, breathe in love and relaxation; as you
exhale, release tension. Allow your consciousness to drift in time
and space.*

(Long pause.)

*Find yourself standing at the foot of a flight of stairs that leads
up to a beautiful temple. At the top of the stairs is a magnificent being
of light welcoming you home. You feel at peace and in awe of the radi-
ance emanating from the temple. You slowly walk up the stairs.*

*As you enter the temple you feel surges of energy rushing
through you. You are led into a room where there are several beings
waiting for you. They are teachers that will help you with your healings. Spend some time getting to know them. Ask them to help you
and guide you. Let them teach you how to proceed.*

(Pause.)

*Thank them and know that they are always there for you. Gen-
tly bring yourself back to present moment focus.*

When you meditate, continue bonding with your teachers.
Relax and ask to be used as a channel for healing energy. Open
yourself up so you can receive that healing energy; relax as
much as possible, and feel the energy flow through you. Practice opening your head and heart and allow the energy to flow
through you. When you heal, you usually send the energy out
through your hands. As the energy begins to flow, your hands
may begin to feel warm or hot.

Once you feel the energy running through you, begin running your hands over your body, keeping your hands a few
inches above your body. Let yourself feel the energy. As much

as possible, simply allow it to flow. Imagine a faucet being turned on and mentally open it more and more until it is fully open. Use mental imagery; see the energy coming in through the top of your head and coming out of your hands. Picture yourself as an empty vessel being filled with a golden light. See the light flowing out of you and filling the world.

Continue practicing during your meditations until you feel comfortable and can sense the energy running fairly easily. When you feel comfortable, begin working with a partner. Take turns working on one another. Start by having one person sit in a straightback chair or a short stool. A stool makes it easier to access his or her back and various power points.

Start by standing behind the person with your hands slightly raised. Quietly say a prayer. Ask to be used as an instrument of love and light. Some people say a favorite prayer. I say a simple one such as:

> *Great Spirit, Creator, please use me as an instrument for your healing energy. May I be a clear channel of your love and light. May those who come before me be reminded of their perfection and may it manifest now. I give thanks for your help, and I call upon those healing beings of light that assist me to be present now.*

When you feel the energy begin to run, start clearing your partner's aura by gently moving your hands over the person's body, a few inches above the surface. One of my teachers compared this to stroking a cat. Let your own style develop. Some people are energetic, waving their hands around, etc., and others are more subdued. Pay special attention to the person's head and feet.

When you are done with the aura, again stand behind the person. Get centered and mentally ask your healers where you need to work first. For me the areas that need the healing energy feel different, at times they seem hot and at others, empty. Trust your instincts and let your hands move over the person's body, lingering wherever they want. Gently work on the person's power points. Let your intuition guide you.

When you've finished, again stand behind the person and say a silent prayer. Close the person's aura by moving your hands from the feet up to the head. I then place my hands gently on the shoulders and send my love. When I am done I tell the person to stand up, and I give him or her a hug.

At times when I am working on people I will get impressions or information. It can be as simple as suggesting they drink more water or change their diet. If it feels appropriate, I pass along these messages.

When you are doing hands-on healing, it is important not to touch the person's body. Most states have strict laws regulating spiritual healing. Unless you have a massage license you can get in trouble by touching the person. This is unfortunate because I often feel moved to rub a certain place on a person's body or move them in a certain way. If I know the person, I will do this anyway, but you could get in trouble with the legal system by doing this. Be sure to check your local regulations.

When I first began healing people during my church's healing service, I felt nothing was happening. Yet week after week people would come to me to work on them. Healing is so subjective, my mind couldn't conceive of the possibility that it might be real. Don't listen to your head; follow your heart.

I enjoy healing because I feel good afterward. It is a wonderful way to share your love. You can also use these techniques on your pets and plants. When I prepare a meal for myself or a friend, I send healing energy into the food. Experiment with this energy; let it teach you. Its uses are endless.

ABSENTEE HEALING

You can also heal people at a distance. Time and space have no meaning when you enter a meditative state. At the level of spirit, everything is one. You can easily do absentee healing in a meditation. Go into an altered state, relax, and call upon your healers. See the person in your mind, greet him or her, and ask permission to begin your work. If you receive it, begin the healing with a prayer. The process is similar to hands-on healing.

Mentally look at the people you heal. Move them around so you can view all parts of their bodies. You can create a laboratory with all sorts of equipment to help you if you like. At times I have used cosmic vacuum cleaners, magic elixirs, and anything else that seemed appropriate or necessary. Visualize them surrounded in light or see healing beings working on them. If you prefer, imagine yourself standing behind them as they sit on your healing stool. Then proceed as you would if they were physically present.

Prayer is another form of absentee healing. Ask the universe to heal the people or ask that healing energy be sent to them.

EXERCISES

1. Buy two small plants that are easy to care for and are of the same size. Take care of them in the same fashion. Choose one of them and send it healing energy at least three times a week. Do this for about a month and notice how much better that plant looks, even though your other treatments of the plants were equal.

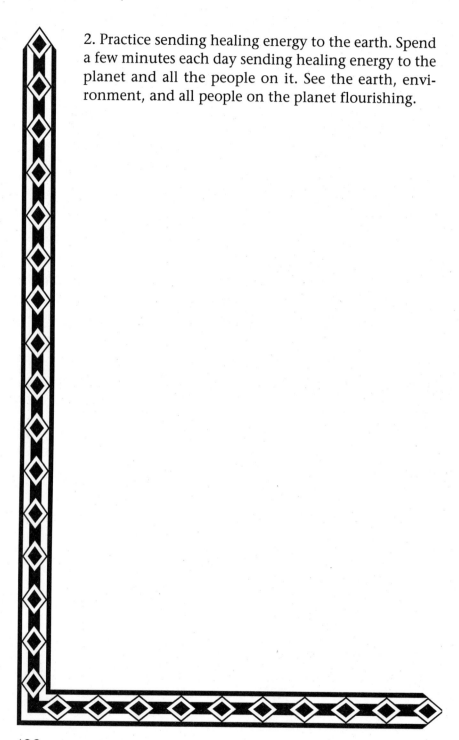

2. Practice sending healing energy to the earth. Spend a few minutes each day sending healing energy to the planet and all the people on it. See the earth, environment, and all people on the planet flourishing.

3. Send healing energies to all the places on this planet that are experiencing turmoil. See those places healed of war, famine, and natural disasters.

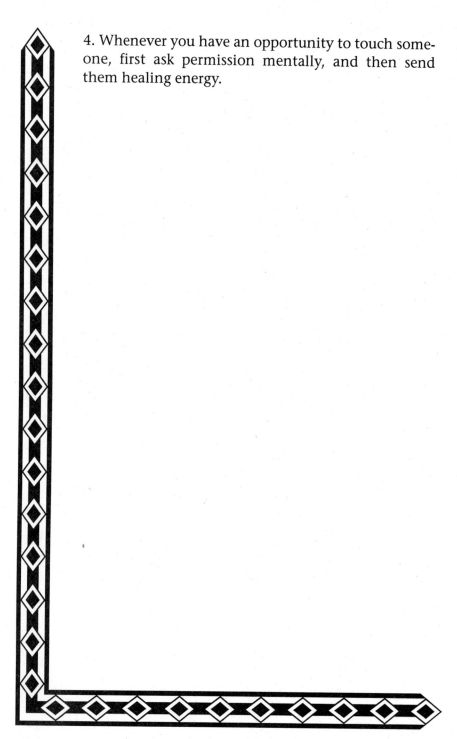

4. Whenever you have an opportunity to touch someone, first ask permission mentally, and then send them healing energy.

NOTES

191

CHAPTER TWELVE

LUCID DREAMING

The young girl awoke when she heard a voice gently calling, "Fawn Eyes." She looked around to see who was calling her, but saw no one. She felt sad as she drifted back to sleep; the only one who ever called her that name was dead. She missed Grandmother so. All the children missed the old woman. There wasn't anyone to tell the little ones stories anymore. She fell asleep thinking about the many days she had spent at Grandmother's feet. Now that hearth was empty, and it saddened her.

She found herself walking along a path near the river. It was early fall and as the morning mist rose off the river, it seemed to have a life of its own. It danced and swirled as the sun tried to shine weakly through it. She noticed there was someone walking along the path with her so she turned to see who it was.

"Welcome, Fawn Eyes," said Grandmother.

The young girl raced to embrace her. Tears of joy streamed down her face, and then she remembered. She stepped back and asked, "Am I dead?"

"No, little one, we are in the dream time. What are dreams but stories the Great Spirit tells us at night?"

"Then why are you here, Grandmother?" asked the girl.

"Do you remember a day long ago when we went for a walk on the river?"

"How could I forget? You told the boys that one of them was going to be the most powerful chief and spiritual leader our people had ever known. After that, they treated one another with honor and respect for fear of offending the chief," replied the girl.

"Yes, except for the lost soul who decided he was the one. It was sad to watch him lose his soul. Do you remember what I told you, Fawn Eyes?" asked the old one.

"No, Grandmother," answered the girl.

"I told you that you would be a great storyteller. It is almost time. You will become a woman in a few weeks and it is time that you begin your work."

"But how, Grandmother? I only know your stories. Why would our people trust me with the little ones?"

"Because you will earn that respect," said the old woman.

At that moment, the girl noticed a white wolf standing next to Grandmother. She looked at the wolf first with fear, then respect. With sudden knowing, she said, "You were the girl with the wolf, weren't you?"

"Yes I was, little one. The wolf has always helped our people to learn about harmony and balance. Wolves are fierce warriors yet when they mate, it is for life. To them the pack is family and is honored. They live in harmony with all beings. To have one as a friend is both an honor and a responsibility not to be taken lightly."

The wolf came and stood by the girl. Timidly she reached out and stroked his neck; he turned and licked her hand. She knelt down and embraced him. In that instant she felt powerful love and strength.

The old one stood and watched, nodding her head with approval. "Everyone has their own path, little one. Yours is not the same as mine, nor should it be. I found my power by saving the life of this wolf; you must find your own act of power. I will continue to help you in the dream time. We will visit again very soon, little one."

It was still dark when the young woman awoke. She thought about Grandmother. What great act of power could she do? For a moment she felt hopeless, she had no idea what she could do. Then she remembered Grandmother telling her that each challenge came with an answer and a gift attached to it. She merely had to wait and an answer would come.

Her life went on as it always had except she looked forward to the coming of night. She loved her nightly visits with Grandmother. They talked about many things but whenever she started to ask about her act of power, she would wake up.

After many months Grandmother announced one night that this would be their last visit together in the dream time. The young woman protested and the old one held her hand up and said, "Little one, I have taught you all I know. You are a woman now. It is time for you to claim your power and begin your life's work."

"But how, Grandmother?" cried the girl. "I still don't know what my act of power is."

The old woman smiled at her and said, "The greatest act of power anyone can make is to step into her sacred center and be herself."

And the young woman woke up.

While I was studying with Miguel, I had incredibly vivid dreams. A great deal of information can be gained from your dreams. While you sleep your conscious mind is absent, so it is easier to gain information that might run contrary to your conscious beliefs. The symbolism in dreams is rich and varied. When you learn to dream lucidly and can guide your dreams, the possibilities are limitless.

Lucid dreamers are people who are able to wake up in their dreams while remaining asleep. They are then able to control their dreams. Lucid dreaming is a skill that takes a great deal of patience and practice to master. Whether or not you ever master lucid dreaming, dreams are wonderful tools and great fun.

They enable you to awaken your spirit body. When you are able to master your dreams, it becomes much easier to travel and gather information from ethereal levels while you sleep at night. Dreaming adds a new dimension to your spiritual self.

Becoming lucid in dreams is as important as becoming lucid in life. When you become conscious of your spiritual nature and realize that you are not your physical body, you wake up in life. You realize that you are a spiritual being, yet you remain in your body and alive on this planet. Once you master this ability, you can create your life in a much more joyous and fulfilling manner.

The first thing you must achieve if you are to become a lucid dreamer is the ability to easily remember your dreams. You dream constantly. Each night you must be able to recall all of your dreams as vividly as possible. To make this process as simple as possible, keep a dream journal. For years I kept a notebook and pencil near my bed so I could write down my dreams during the night or first thing in the morning.

Before I went to bed, I would remind myself that I was going to remember my dreams. At first I reminded myself to remember one of my dreams. When that became easy, I affirmed that I would remember two dreams. Once I was comfortable with that, I reminded myself to remember all my dreams each night. Make sure you write down your dreams as soon as you awaken or you will forget them, no matter how vivid they are.

The next step is to begin programming your dreams. Begin by telling yourself that you will have a dream about a specific topic and that you will remember and understand it. Start with something simple, a topic that you are familiar with and interested in. It may take a few nights for you to succeed, but you will succeed if you continue. Enjoy the process. Learning how to work with your dreams can be a great deal of fun, so relax. Let this be a playful process that you can truly enjoy. Your mind is much more likely to cooperate when you are having fun.

If you have a dream about the subject but don't understand it, ask for a dream the next night to explain it. Keep working with your dreams until you are comfortable with the process and until you succeed on a regular basis. Once you are able to do this, you can use your dreams to access information on almost any subject. If you have a problem in your life, you can ask to have a dream about its solution. Our minds are incredibly creative and when we are in an altered state we can access information from anywhere in the universe.

The first time I taught a women's group on the goddess energy, I had no idea how to structure the class or what my focus should be. I asked for a dream before I went to sleep. The next morning I awoke with a memory of a series of dreams I had years ago when I was studying with Sarita. She and Miguel had come to me at night and taught me a great deal of information. I had forgotten the dreams. In the process of remembering, I gathered much information about women and spirituality.

For seven nights immediately following one of my initiations with Miguel, I had a series of dreams. I wasn't sure what was happening. The meaning of the dreams wasn't clear, and I woke up each morning exhausted. The morning of the seventh night, as soon as I woke up, I heard a voice telling me to write them down. In my usual fashion I procrastinated. The voice kept haunting me until I finally wrote down the content of my dreams. When I was finished, I was amazed. I had a series of exercises that were the basis of the first set of classes that I taught. I later expanded the information and wrote a book based on that information.

The information you receive in your dreams often depends as much on the questions you ask as it does upon your dedication. Be wary of asking yourself "why" questions, which tend to create an endless circle of thoughts that inevitably lead you to feeling negative about yourself. I tell my clients that the answer to "why" is "why not." When you ask yourself why something happened, your mind will always come up with an answer, but it will frequently explain why you are defective or undeserving.

If you ask yourself how you can change something or what you can do or learn, you will get much more useful information. That is true for all areas of your life. The questions you ask yourself control how you feel about yourself and your world. If you ask why something happened to you, the question implies that something is wrong with you, and that God is punishing you. The answers to those questions will certainly not make you feel better about yourself. Always ask questions that will help you grow and feel good about yourself. Feeling bad about yourself does not help you grow in any way; it only adds to your shame, which tends to keep you stuck.

When you program your dreams, ask yourself questions that will help you feel better and allow you to grow emotionally and spiritually: What can I do to improve ___? What can I do to learn ___? How can I increase ___? How can I change ___? I would like more information about ___. Where does the magic lie for me in ___? Help me change ___. If you want to do something specific like lose weight or quit smoking, ask yourself how you could do it and enjoy the process. Stress concepts like "enjoy the process," "do it easily," "succeed effortlessly," etc. After all, life is about having fun.

Play with your dreams for a while. I find my dreams become extremely vivid when an emotional issue is coming up for me or when I am about to make a major shift in my life. Sometimes I merely need information on a subject, and I receive it in my dreams before I even know I need it. Avoid depending on dream interpretation books. Everyone has their own unique symbols. Water may mean one thing to you and something entirely different to someone else. If you are using a book, you are interpreting your dreams according to the author's symbols. There really are no indisputable archetype symbols inherent to human beings; we create our own. If you are unsure of the meaning of your dream, ask for a dream the next night to explain it. Your answers always lie within yourself.

Even though I now seldom program for specific dreams, I always ask for guidance and direction before I go to sleep. When I first started this book, I found myself having problems writing. I had laughed when people talked about writer's block because writing had always been so easy for me. For weeks at a time I was unable to force myself to sit down at my computer. Finally, I started asking for help before I went to bed. I assumed that I would begin receiving information on the various chapters. Instead, I started getting excited about writing a mystery novel. I began dreaming about the mystery night after night. I got so excited about writing that book that I was able to easily complete this one. My rational linear mind never would have come up with that solution, but it worked. Dreams are like that: the solutions are effective, yet seldom in the form we expect.

Let your dreams unfold in their own manner. The more open you are to receiving information, the easier it will be for you to accept it. When I first started thinking about a mystery, my initial reaction was to reject the idea. My first thought was that I didn't know how to write fiction. As I became more open to the idea, the more intriguing it became. And it worked! The rest of this book flowed easily. As for the success of the mystery, I am not sure—time will tell.

Once you are comfortable playing with your dreams, begin to program yourself to become conscious while you are still asleep in your dreams. Remind yourself before you go to bed that you will wake up in your dreams while your body remains asleep. It may take time, but it will happen. The first time I realized I was conscious while I was asleep I was so excited I immediately woke up. It took me weeks to have another lucid dream.

You can trick yourself into waking up by programming yourself to look at your hands in your dreams. I have had people tell me that they have become lucid dreamers by looking into a mirror in their dreams. The traditional way to become lucid in your dreams is to look at your hands while bringing them up to your face. Concentrating on our hands and looking in mirrors are unusual events in dreams, so they tend to jar us awake while we stay in the dream.

Once you are lucid in your dream, you can do whatever you want within it. I had one student who had always been a lucid dreamer. He could fly and create anything he wanted during that state. His frustration was that he was unable to do the same things while in his waking states. Eventually, he did become adept at creating what he wanted while awake; it just took practice. The same thing is true with lucid dreaming: You will succeed, as long as you keep trying.

Once you are able to dream lucidly on a regular basis, you can decide what you would like to do in your dreams. If you would like to go to a specific location, remind yourself of that before you go to sleep. Lucid dreaming is one of the precursors of being able to bio-locate, or to be in two places at once. In your dreams there are no boundaries—you can do anything you choose as long as you can imagine it. If you would like to go to Paris or the moon, you can go in your dreams and actually be there. I have known of people who have gone to a location first in their dreams and then later physically. The details of the location were the same and without the dream they would have had no way of knowing them.

I have had lucid dreams of the future, but did not understand them at the time. Later, when I began to experience the events of the dreams, I understood fully what the dreams had been about. It is an unusual experience. Before I understood about lucid dreaming I found it frightening. Now I smile whenever I start to live my dreams.

Dreams can help you live your fantasies. You can use them to learn more about yourself and your purpose for being here. You can use them to help you love and accept your entire self. You can also use them to have fun and enjoy life.

EXERCISES

1. Keep a dream journal and see how it corresponds to what is going on in your life. Over time, do you see any patterns?

2. Before you go to bed each night, mentally review your day in reverse. Release any emotions or judgments you have about yourself, others, or the day. If you feel you made any mistakes, correct them and forgive yourself. If you review and release your day before you go to bed, you won't need to do it in your dreams. Notice how your dreams change when you remember to do this.

3. Begin using your dreams to assist you in changing any patterns or behaviors that stop you from living your life fully. Ask for a dream that will show you what beliefs, thoughts, or behaviors you need to change to create a life filled with everything you could possibly wish for. Then ask for a dream to show you how to do that. You can use your dreams to create magic in your life.

NOTES

▲▲▲ FINAL NOTE ▲▲▲

I hope that as you have read this book and experimented with the exercises, you have come to know yourself a little bit better. The exercises were designed to act as a unit. They lead you slowly away from your rational linear mind into your heart or sacred center. They will help you find that sacred center for yourself.

I could write volumes about my philosophy and observations on how this universe operates, but that isn't what this path is about. It is about you making your own observations and finding your own truths. As you find your own power and center, you will know the truth for yourself and have the courage to live it.

This path is one that is filled with dignity and respect. It is based upon self-love, upon honoring the individual, and upon the freedom we each have to choose our own path. The only requirements on this path are the courage to know yourself and the perseverance necessary to find your sacred self.

This process will continue to unfold in your life if you are willing to let it. Dedicate your life to learning how to love yourself unconditionally. That alone will create miracles in your life.

Feel your feelings, be gentle with yourself, and be loving. It all sounds easy, but when fear rears it ugly head, our ability to be loving is no longer the issue. Survival becomes the only focus and love ceases to exist. Love is the only thing that is real so walk through the fear, but don't react to it. Let the fear pass through you and don't feed it by giving it your attention. Love even your fear, and it will serve as a guidepost that lets you know that you are getting closer to the truth.

Every morning ask yourself how you can love yourself unconditionally that day and enjoy the process of loving. Ask yourself what miracles will happen that day, what new thing you will learn to help you be more loving and more open. Focus on your joy, and you will get more joy. Start each day by feeling grateful that you are alive, and you will have a day filled with love. End each day the same way and you will soon be living your dreams.

Allow yourself to open up to a world based on the foundation of freedom and love, rather than one based on limitations and fear. This world is filled with miracles and unicorns if we are willing to see them. See your own perfection and live always in love.

In love and light,

Susan

Author's note: Readers may also contact Dr. Gregg by electronic mail. Her address is: 75302.50@compuserve.com.

▲▲▲ GLOSSARY ▲▲▲

Altar: An object used in the performance of sacred rites or ceremonies upon which ritual tools and items are placed. A sacred place.

Attention: The place where we direct our energy. What we choose to observe and/or focus on.

Aura: Energetically the human form is that of a luminescent egg made up of energy fibers. The aura is the part of that energy field that is closest to the body.

Brain waves: The brain gives off a variety of electrical impulses. They are generally broken down into four wave lengths and each one is indicative of a certain type of mental activity.

> **Beta** (14Hz and up): This wave length is most associated with physical activity and stressful situations. At these higher levels the body begins to produce hormones such as adrenaline which are harmful to the body when experienced on a regular basis.

> **Alpha** (8 to 14Hz): This wave length is associated with relaxation and light meditative states. At this wave length your body begins to produce hormones that relax the body.

> **Theta** (4 to 8 Hz): This wave length is associated with deep trance states and deep meditations. It is also the first stage of sleep.

> **Delta** (below 4 Hz): The wave length associated with an unconscious state of mind.

Catch the energy: A phrase that is used to describe a person's ability to understand and interpret information from the ethereal levels.

Channel: A person or being who has the ability to act as a conductor of energy.

Discipline: The act of taking deliberate actions. Planned actions designed to achieve a desired result.

Dreamer: A person who accesses information from the ethereal level in the form of pictures.

Dreamtime: An alternative reality we enter as we dream. It is a way of using dreams to access information or to use the energy you access in your daily life in some way.

Duality: The belief that there is a separation from the God-source creates the belief in the illusion of duality or the concept of opposites. Examples: black and white, good and evil, right and wrong.

Ego: The part of a human being most closely aligned with the mind. It believes it is a physical body. It can be either a hindrance or a tool depending upon how it is used. If it is used as an interface with physical reality, it is a wonderful tool. When it is in charge of a person's life, it has a very negative influence because it closes down the person's connection to his or her spiritual self.

Energy: Available power; what the universe is made of.

Ethereal: An energy level. In a sense it is a buffer zone between the physical and spiritual levels.

Goddess energy: The feminine aspect of God. I think of it as an energy that is all inclusive, gentle, and loving. It is the energy that gave birth to the universe. As it was worshipped years ago, it was exclusionary as was the concept of God in its male aspect. True goddess energy excludes no one, it is the universe in all its aspects.

Handling power: A person's ability to channel power. The act of channeling power in order to transform it—to use it for healing or manifesting.

Intention: A person's aim or purpose, that which the person plans to achieve by his or her actions.

Invocation: A ceremony in which all the energy of the participants and the leader is focused and directed for a specific purpose. The powers of the "gods" and the elements are also invoked for that specific goal. It is a cermony which is not done lightly. A person might use this ceremony once in a lifetime. It is created by using a specific series of power moves and once the energy is at its peak, it is released and then directed toward the goal.

Lucid dreaming: The ability to maintain conscious awareness in one's dreams.

Magic: Power that has been transformed into a physical manifestion.

Meditation: An altered state of consciousness, a state of mind in which the individual produces alpha brain waves. Because it's a relaxed state of mind, the mind may continue to chatter but the body feels relaxed.

Nagual: A person of power and wisdom. Most Naguals are sorcerers, the magicians of the spiritual realms. The tradition goes back to the ancient Toltecs, Aztecs, and Mayans.

Personal importance: Ego in the negative sense.

Personal power: The amount of power a person is able to handle or channel.

Power: Energy that has been captured and is in the process of being transformed into something. The ability to take action.

Power points: A focal point within a person's body, a place where several of our energy filaments come together.

Power spots: Areas on the earth where there is a concentration of energy; similar to power points on the human body.

Power moves: Physical movements of the body designed to facilitate the person in increasing the amount of power he or she can handle. An example of ancient power moves is tai chi.

Protector: An energy being whose purpose is to keep us safe as we explore the universe beyond our conscious awareness.

Psychic surgery: A profound method of spiritual healing. The practitioner actually cuts into the person's energy body and realigns the physical structure.

Sacred: A person, place, thing, or location secured against violation or interference.

Sacred place: A place that is treated with reverence and respect. A place of power; a place where power is easy accessed.

Sacred self: Also known as inner self, essential self, essence, and true self.

Shadow: Those energies that exist in the darkness. Shadows are a door to the ethereal; they give our world form. Remember darkness does not necessarily mean negative.

Shadow self: The parts of our personality or behaviors that we refuse to acknowledge to ourselves or to others.

Shaman: A healer of relationships, the relationship you have with your world, yourself, with others in your life, and most importantly, with your spiritual self. They are guides that empower you and help you inf inding your true nature.

Spirit helper: Those energy beings whose pupose is to remind us of our sacred nature. They are often parts of our soul, pieces of ourselves that we are not consciously aware of so they seem to manifest as separate beings.

Stalker: A person who intuitively knows blocks of information from the ethereal level. After a meditation the individual returns with a block of information. The opposite is a dreamer, who has a vision and must then interpret it.

Stalking: The act of watching and pursuing an objective such as a person, place, or thing. It is usually used in assocation with stalking power and moving cautiously.

On the following pages you will find listed, with their current prices, some of the books now available on related subjects. Your book dealer stocks most of these and will stock new titles in the Llewellyn series as they become available. We urge your patronage.

TO GET A FREE CATALOG

You are invited to write for our bi-monthly news magazine/catalog, *Llewellyn's New Worlds of Mind and Spirit*. A sample copy is free, and it will continue coming to you at no cost as long as you are an active mail customer. Or you may subscribe for just $10 in the United States and Canada ($20 overseas, first class mail). Many bookstores also have *New Worlds* available to their customers. Ask for it.

In *New Worlds* you will find news and features about new books, tapes and services; announcements of meetings and seminars; helpful articles; author interviews and much more. Write to:

Llewellyn's New Worlds of Mind and Spirit
P.O. Box 64383-K334, St. Paul, MN 55164-0383, U.S.A.

TO ORDER BOOKS AND TAPES

If your book store does not carry the titles described on the following pages, you may order them directly from Llewellyn by sending the full price in U.S. funds, plus postage and handling (see below).

Credit card orders: VISA, MasterCard, American Express are accepted. Call us toll-free within the United States and Canada at 1-800-THE-MOON.

Special Group Discount: Because there is a great deal of interest in group discussion and study of the subject matter of this book, we offer a 20% quantity discount to group leaders or agents. Our Special Quantity Price for a minimum order of five copies of *Finding the Sacred Self* is $48 cash-with-order. Include postage and handling charges noted below.

Postage and Handling: Include $4 postage and handling for orders $15 and under; $5 for orders *over* $15. There are no postage and handling charges for orders over $100. Postage and handling rates are subject to change. We ship UPS whenever possible within the continental United States; delivery is guaranteed. Please provide your street address as UPS does not deliver to P.O. boxes. Orders shipped to Alaska, Hawaii, Canada, Mexico and Puerto Rico will be sent via first class mail. Allow 4-6 weeks for delivery. **International orders:** Airmail—add retail price of each book and $5 for each non-book item (audiotapes, etc.); Surface mail—add $1 per item.

Minnesota residents add 7% sales tax.

Mail orders to:
Llewellyn Worldwide, P.O. Box 64383-K334, St. Paul, MN 55164-0383,
U.S.A.
For customer service, call (612) 291-1970.

DANCE OF POWER
A Shamanic Journey
by Dr. Susan Gregg

Join Dr. Susan Gregg on her fascinating, real-life journey to find her soul. This is the story of her shamanic apprenticeship with a man named Miguel, a Mexican-Indian Shaman, or "Nagual." As you live the author's personal experiences, you have the opportunity to take a quantum leap along the path toward personal freedom, toward finding your true self, and grasping the ultimate personal freedom—the freedom to choose moment by moment what you want to experience.

Here, in a warm and genuine style, Dr. Gregg details her studies with Miguel, her travel to other realms, and her initiations by fire and water into the life of a "warrior." If you want to understand how you create your own reality—and how you may be wasting energy by resisting change or trying to understand the unknowable—take the enlightening path of the Nagual. Practical exercises at the end of each chapter give you the tools to embark upon your own spiritual quest.

Learn about another way of being ... *Dance of Power* can change your life, if you let it.

0-87542-247-0, 5 1/4 x 8, illus., photos, softbound   **$12.95**

ANIMAL-SPEAK
The Spiritual & Magical Powers of
Creatures Great & Small
by Ted Andrews

The animal world has much to teach us. Some are experts at survival and adaptation, some never get cancer, some embody strength and courage while others exude playfulness. Animals remind us of the potential we can unfold, but before we can learn from them, we must first be able to speak with them.

Now, for perhaps the first time ever, myth and fact are combined in a manner that will teach you how to speak and understand the language of the animals in your life. *Animal-Speak* helps you meet and work with animals as totems and spirits—by learning the language of their behaviors within the physical world. It provides techniques for reading signs and omens in nature so you can open to higher perceptions and even prophecy. It reveals the hidden, mythical and realistic roles of 45 animals, 60 birds, 8 insects and 6 reptiles.

Animals will become a part of you, revealing to you the majesty and divine in all life. They will restore your childlike wonder of the world and strengthen your belief in magic, dreams and possibilities.

0-87542-028-1, 400 pgs., 7 x 10, illus., photos, softcover $17.95

BY OAK, ASH & THORN
Modern Celtic Shamanism
by D. J. Conway
Many spiritual seekers are interested in shamanism because it is a spiritual path that can be followed in conjunction with any religion or other spiritual belief without conflict. Shamanism has not only been practiced by Native American and African cultures—for centuries, it was practiced by the Europeans, including the Celts.

By Oak, Ash and Thorn presents a workable, modern form of Celtic shamanism that will help anyone raise his or her spiritual awareness. Here, in simple, practical terms, you will learn to follow specific exercises and apply techniques that will develop your spiritual awareness and ties with the natural world: shape-shifting, divination by the Celtic Ogham alphabet, Celtic shamanic tools, traveling to and using magick in the three realms of the Celtic otherworlds, empowering the self, journeying through meditation and more.

Shamanism begins as a personal revelation and inner healing, then evolves into a striving to bring balance and healing into the Earth itself. This book will ensure that Celtic shamanism will take its place among the spiritual practices that help us lead fuller lives.

1-56718-166-X, 6 x 9, 320 pp., illus., softcover   **$12.95**